MW00928332

Happily
Ticked
Off

ANDREA R. FRAZER

Copyright © 2015 Andrea R. Frazer

Armonia
Publishing

All rights reserved.
ISBN: 1511446374
ISBN-13: 978-1511446372

Dedication

This is for you, Mamas.

When my son was diagnosed with Tourette Syndrome seven years ago, I encountered loads of disheartening information on the internet about tics, ADHD, OCD and disturbed children with behavior problems.

I found blogs full of victimhood stories and medications gone wrong.

I found a few helpful but ultimately dry informational books written from medical and nutritional viewpoints on how to suppress tics through natural or pharmaceutical means.

What I *didn't* encounter, however, was a book on humor, support and most importantly, hope.

So I wrote one.

This book is not just for mamas dealing with Tourette Syndrome. It's a love letter for all you moms dealing with an unexpected diagnosis. It's the book I wish someone had written for me when I was hopeless, angry, and feeling so very alone.

It's my sincere hope that this mom-moir will serve as one giant hug for your fears. May it whisper into your heart, "You did not cause this disorder. You are strong enough to handle it. Your child is perfect despite some medical challenges. You are not alone. I am here. YOU CAN DO THIS."

For all you mamas out there who are hanging by a thread, I'm asking you to tie a knot and hang on. *Happily Ticked Off* was written for you.

ANDREA R. FRAZER

Table of Contents

ANDREA R. FRAZER

Prologue

Happily TIC-ked Off

"Your son has Tourette Syndrome."

I looked up at a stern woman in her late 30's. She had her arms folded tightly against her heart. (*If* she had a heart. The verdict was still out.) Black and silver hair spilled down her white lab coat, covering up her name tag. "Dr. Badbedside Manners."

Combined with her pale skin and silver jewelry, she looked like a cross between Stevie Nicks and the Bride of Frankenstein. The diagnosis she just handed me didn't make me less terrified of her.

Stop being a wussy," I told myself.

I glanced at the diploma on her wall and collected my thoughts. I had to admit, only a delusional freak would be surprised by her words. After all, my four-year-old had been referred to her only after I had already depleted every cent of my family's HMO deductible on allergy testing, vision tests and more pediatric visits than my son had Scooby Doo band-aids. I was hoping all these visits would provide an answer to why my kid would transition from clearing his throat several times per minute to rolling his eyes side to side in rapid succession.

How I loved the pattern of those eyes on my retro kitty tic-toc clock! The predictable back and forth motion never ceased to instill a profound sense of joy and fun as I sipped my morning coffee and stared at them. Seeing them on my child? Not so much fun. Far from viewing it as kooky and eccentric, those eye rolls inspired nothing less than primal fear.

And anger.

Which... I'm ashamed to say... I took out on the kit-kat clock earlier that morning.

Only a bad mother would take out her irritation on a preschooler. But that cat? She was fair game.

First she lost her tail. Then she was shattered to bits in a moment of pure frustration when my son morphed from eye rolls into unexpected gulps. Those tics, and that cat, had to go.

I tried to squelch the tears brimming behind my eyes. I wish my husband were here to hold my murderous little hand.

He was not. And that stunk.

Perhaps it was because I was alone on that ill-fated day that the revelation hit me so hard. Perhaps if Rex had been there to steady me . . . to wrap me in those strong, lithe arms of his . . . the blow would have felt less intense.

Lucky for me, I recovered quickly. I was the queen of composure.

"Tourette's? You mean... But how...Wah wah *HUH*?"

Dr. Badbedside Manners didn't twitch, and not just because she didn't have Tourette Syndrome. Likely she was used to moms like me. Moms who, despite hope against hope . . . despite seeing the signs themselves for months on end . . . were banking on a different outcome.

I'd hoped to hear he had a vitamin deficiency. Instead, I was handed a nightmare. With nothing more than a few words about this little known syndrome, I was told to come back in six months.

When I called my husband on the car ride home, I had only one statement: "Nicky has Tourette Syndrome."

My husband had only one answer. "What happened to the kitchen clock?"

I hung up the phone and sobbed like a baby.

And that, my friends, was the beginning of a hellish six years.

Determined that no mama should go through what I did, I wrote a book.

This is the story I wish someone had written for me. My hopes are that it saves not only people's sanities, and their marriages, but also perfectly innocent kit-cat clocks. No time-piece, no matter how annoying, deserves that kind of brutality.

This is my journey.

This is my story.

If you're up upset at your child's diagnosis, whether it be T.S., Autism or some other spectrum disorder, I want you to know I've been there.

I'll have you Happily Ticked Off in no time. How about we start with a few facts I wish someone had sent to me during the first lonely, dark leg of this journey.

FACTS and HOPE

Tics or a T.S. Diagnosis

If you've picked up this book there's a decent chance your child has recently begun to tic or has just been diagnosed with Tourette Syndrome. You're pretty ticked off.

My son was diagnosed at 4 years with T.S.. He's now 12. He's well-adjusted, funny and loaded with friends. With the right plan and perspective your child can have a similar outcome.

Freak-out time

You want to believe me, but you're still panicked. Second only to dismay over this new diagnosis is the regret that you didn't invest stock in the Kleenex Corporation. You can't stop crying.

Neither could I. I'd sob to myself, my friends, my family – even bewildered gas station cashiers who simply wanted to sell me a Diet Coke – not hear a dissertation on the boring clinical definition of Tourette's.

Boring Clinical Definition of Tourette's

Named for Georges Gilles de la Tourette in 1885, Tourette's consists of both vocal and physical tics that wax and wane in nature and last up to one year. I'll get into more detail later, but for now, let's move on to something you can really relate to... like whining!

"What happened to my perfect little boy?" was my broken record, twenty four hours a day. No one had an answer, but I have one for you: nothing has happened to your child. Your child is still perfect. Just hang tight. I survived this initial scary period and you will, too. I promise.

It's Not Fair

You know life isn't perfect and this condition could be a heck of a lot worse, but you're still upset. You can't see the big picture when you're living the unsettling, fearful present.

In the subconscious recesses of my mind, I knew Tourette's would one day be viewed as a present, but that didn't keep me from spending the next seven years looking for the gift receipt. "Thank you, but no thank you. I appreciate the thought, but I'd like to return this for something else. Perhaps a good case of musical genius, a pitcher's arm, or the ability to burp the Ave Maria."

The Symptoms

Maybe you have no official label yet, but something is wrong and you're freaking out. What you used to see as your child's occasional quirky habits has morphed into unrelenting blinks, eye rolls, jerky head nods and spastic facial grimaces.

It's hard to watch your child go through this, but stay strong. Tics are like visiting in-laws who invade over Thanksgiving – they're annoying, can drive you to drink, and just when you get used to them they take off as quickly as they arrived.

The Nature of Tics

Like the departure of your extended family, you feel immense relief that the tics are gone. But Christmas is just around the corner. You have a deep sense of foreboding that those tics – and those in-laws – will be back. What if this time they bring friends?

It's true that after a quiet period, tics often return. Sometimes kids exhibit the same tic as before and add a different one. Sometimes one tic goes completely away only to be replaced by a new one altogether. Like your Aunt Sally, tics are eccentric and always changing. At least they don't wear housecoats and smell like old musk.

The Evil of the Internet

You are a normally well-balanced person, but you begin to worry something more serious is at the root. After searching like a mad woman on the internet, you're bombarded with hundreds of frightening outcomes for your child.

Seriously, this isn't helpful. Turn off the computer. (Okay, fine. Don't listen to me. Keep researching deep into the night like a crazed lunatic. I did the same. But let me reiterate THIS ISN'T HELPFUL.)

Perspective Lost

You begin to slide down the rabbit hole. In that dark pit, you become dizzy and disoriented. You lose perspective. You go to dismal places like brain cancer.

It's not brain cancer. Your overworked mama brain, however, is spinning like a jacked up tilt-o-whirl on truck stop java. Stop the ride! Minus some extra dopamine, your child's brain is perfectly healthy.

Perspective Gained

In most cases – as will be the journey relayed in this book – T.S. and tics remain mild to moderate until adulthood. Then like your wonky Uncle Donny and Cousin Frankie, they disappear altogether. (Pssst...it's such a relief no one goes looking for them!)

Focusing on positive outcomes can really keep your negative thinking in check. If you can't instantly change the tics, change your thinking.

Severe Cases & Seeking Medical Attention

In extreme scenarios (which you'll get plenty of if you don't listen to me and scour the internet into all hours of the night) you'll find cases of children screeching, spitting, jerking and having to be hospitalized. This is rare. The thought, however, is understandably upsetting. As with mild tics, it's always advisable to seek medical attention.

*Start with your primary care physician who can then refer you to a neurologist if needed. Don't be surprised if, after seeing your pediatrician, they seem very unconcerned. Your "emergency tic OH MY GOD **IT COULD BE SEIZURES**" situation is very commonplace to doctors. It can take months to see a neurologist. I say this not to frustrate you but to assure you that your child isn't the first one to ever experience this.*

Identifying the Triggers (as well as the ever-important legal term known as "Butt Coverage").

I am not a doctor. I am not a certified nutritionist. I am not a psychologist. I am, however, a mother who has been dealing with Tourette's for over eight years. This book will share what has eased my son's symptoms, what has exasperated them, what has eased my symptoms of panic, and what has exasperated them.

Even if your child is dealing with an acute onslaught of tics, the present doesn't need to indicate the future. Many mothers, with time and patience, have pinpointed triggers for their children's symptoms. Once these triggers were eliminated, they were able to drastically reduce the tics.

Medication vs. Supplements

You are not a patient person. You want to stop the tics *this instant* and are bent on getting a prescription for Clonodine or Tenex quicker than you can say Giles De la

Tourette. You want a quick fix, and medication is your answer.

That is a very personal choice and I support you on that journey. I have considered this possibility for my own son, especially now that he's in those tumultuous 'tween years. I'll keep you updated on this at my blog, www.HappilyTickedOff.com.

Self-Esteem

Many of you will opt for a more natural route to easing tics, but you worry about your child's self-esteem while you work out a game plan. You don't want him teased. Your heart breaks that some nasty kid will poke fun at his arm-thrusting tic.

I understand your concern. I was crushed at the prospect of some bully tormenting my baby. But I set my emotions aside and focused on a more important reality: Cruel kids are going to tease other children whether or not those children have tics. My son's heart, character and personality would define him, not his tics.

"That's easier said than done," you might wail.

To that I will respond with a resounding, "Duh." But with practice, you'll learn to focus on your child's strengths, not his tics.

Mild Tics/Mild Annoyance

If your child has mild tics, there's a good chance he doesn't notice them or isn't bothered by them.

This last statement is hard to believe, but it's true. Your kid might be happily watching Spongebob, coughing like a bronchitis-stricken seal six times a minute, and his only complaint at the end of the show will be, "Mommy, I could really go for a bologna and cheese sandwich."

Your Child's Life Is Not Over

To highly tuned-in mamas like yourselves, your children's inability to be affected by tics is baffling, because every minor gulp, throat clear and tongue click will be magnified into **LOUD! RICOCHETING! EXPLOSIONS!** They will boom like a foghorn in your ringing ears, taunting you that *your child's life is O-V-E-R.*

Your child's life is far from over. Tics or T.S. is not a death sentence. The only thing that needs to die is your old vision of what you thought your child's life would look like. He can experience as much success as a non-ticking child.

It's Not Your Fault

I'd lie if I said I have 100% embraced T.S., but with some experience under my belt, I have better days than worse days. I might make my kid eat broccoli on purpose, but I didn't give him T.S. on purpose. I don't blame myself for his condition.

Whether your child has a unique case of T.S. or he had a genetic pre-disposition to it, stop feeling guilty about it. Focus instead on passing down other incredible gifts to your child, such as the ability to stay curious about life, the ability to love, the ability to experience endless joy and the ability to tell a killer joke. (Never underestimate that last talent. It far surpasses tics any day of the week.)

You Feel Like You Could Die

"I'm devastated," you might moan. "Acceptance is about as likely to happen for me as winning the Lottery. And frankly, I'd trade in tics for a million dollar jackpot any day of the week."

Unlike tics that often appear out of nowhere, transformation doesn't happen overnight. You'll need time to both accept this crazy syndrome as well as come up with a protocol that will lessen your child's symptoms. You need to be patient.

Patience-Schmatience

"How can I be patient?" You'll snap. "As if I didn't already have the stress of bills, housecleaning, work and a husband who, for the record, seems eerily unshaken by these tics and has no idea why I'm freaking out, I now have to listen to lip smacking five times a minute for three hours straight?!?!"

To this I'll respond, "Patience comes when you stop paying such close attention."

And to that you will respond with something that sounds like "I hate you, you self-righteous –know-it- all- bad-bad-lying-liar-who-lies writer lady."

Go ahead. I can take it. I can also handle your protests about how you've tried not to pay attention to your kid's noises, but you can't help yourself.

It Gets Better

"There he goes again!" you'll complain, as you read this introduction and scan for tics with the obsession of a hound dog sniffing out convicts. (Congrats on the multi-tasking, btw.)

To all this I will heartily add that I have been there. I get it. It will get better.

No one Understands!

You very likely will roll your eyes, wondering for a brief moment if you yourself have tics but then realize you're simply being catty to me which, again, I forgive you. You will then convince yourself that no one else could possibly understand your frustration and hopelessness.

But I do understand it. I have been locked in car rides through the desert where no amount of country music could drown out my son's post swimming throat clears. For days afterwards, similar to Old Faithful, I couldn't help watching and waiting for his well-timed and unremitting eruptions.

Other People Don't Notice Tics Like You Do

"Old Faithful is an excellent analogy," you agree, "because everyone is going to stare at him in public – clapping and jeering at this unique and boisterous spectacle."

Unlike visiting a national monument, most people are not interested in the incredible national treasure that is your child. They simply will not notice the minor sounds and vocal movements. (Note: As a narcissist in transition, I am constantly working on that last piece of advice myself.)

No Room for Fear

But I'm terrified he will be ostracized by his peers! What if he be barks after busses and curses the F-Word in circle time!"

Get that fear a muzzle, because like your bad high school boyfriend, it lies like a rug. (For the record, less than 10% of T.S. kids uncontrollably curse. So let's keep this worry in check and take it one step at a time, okay?)

Moms' Survival Tactics

You consider getting earplugs but figure good mothers would never avoid the sounds of their children. You berate yourself for finding excuses to fold laundry to avoid watching your daughter blink and jaw thrust over her chapter book.

One of the best mothers I know rearranged her houseplants so she wouldn't have to see her daughter nod her head over and over at the breakfast table.

Many people would call foliage adjustment poor parenting.

I call it brilliant. It's a perfectly acceptable survival mechanism.

Perseverance

By now you're not sure if I've completely lost my mind, but a small part of your brain is telling you I might be making sense. You agree to try out a little patience, but aren't sure how to start.

How about right now?

Take a deep breath.

Tell yourself that for just this moment everything is going to be fine.

All you have to do is be your child's mother – in whatever state he or she is in.

Tell yourself that you don't have all the answers, but you're going to try your best to take it one step at a time.

Take another deep breath.

And now allow me to share a little story with you as you take your first jaunt down that long and windy road of patience. This inspirational tale is one I heard long before my Nicky was diagnosed with Tourette's. On rough days for me – which at the beginning were every day – its encouraging message would soothe my brain like a good cabernet.

Side Note: **Drinking**

During the early days, a bad cabernet worked just as well. If you, too, find yourself drinking a bit more to calm down at the end of the day, you wouldn't be the first frazzled mama to do so. But I encourage you to keep it in check. T.S. isn't going away anytime soon. Does your ticking son really need to be flanked by a slurring mother hopped up on Two Buck Chuck? And really, it's going to be hard enough to find time to cook healthier meals, schedule in more exercise, shop for supplements and fit in a meditation schedule. Combined with AA meetings, you'll soon find yourself ticking, too. Careful, okay?

Now, back to our regular scheduled programming of inspirational story-telling.

Story Time

One of my favorite all time stories about special needs is called "Welcome to Holland." I took the liberty of adapting it for my experience with Tourette's.

One day a family of five boarded a plane headed for London. It was winter, which meant their luggage was filled with sweaters, thick wooly socks, mittens and scarves. The mother, who had dreamed of this vacation ever since she had children ten years prior, had planned out the entire trip in painstaking detail. They would have tea near Buckingham Palace after shopping at Harrods. They would tour the Tate and take a family Christmas photo in front of Big Ben. They would catch a show in the West End and go to mass at St. Paul's.

After two hours on the plane, she looked over at her three children who had magically fallen asleep in the seats between herself and her handsome husband. She grabbed her mate's strong hand, smiling at how perfectly everything had fallen into place.

At one point the captain's voice streamed over the P.A. system. "Ladies and Gentlemen, thank you for flying with us today. Due to some unexpected orders from the ground crew, this plane will no longer be flying to England. We will be changing directions entirely and landing in Africa. I can't give you much information other than we cannot alter our course. You will have no choice but to make the best of the new arrangement. We're not sure when we'll be able to get you back home but you all seem like capable people who can wing it just fine. So, with that in mind, enjoy your new destination!"

Understandably, the mother was horrified at this news. Her husband remained cool and collected. She was both grateful, and horrified, that he wasn't as freaked out as she was. How could he be so calm??! How could this enormous error happen? She wasn't prepared for this abrupt switch of plans! This was not the way her dream vacation was supposed to go. The remainder of the flight was spent in abject misery as she ruminated, sulked, cried, moaned, hollered and generally cursed her fate.

By the time the plane landed, she was in quite a quandary. While this was one of the most unsettling experiences of her life, she also knew that falling apart would not help anyone. She'd have to be strong for the kids. She'd have to lean on her husband when she could. But mostly, she'd have to lean on herself. She'd attempt to make the best of it. What choice did she have?

Once on the ground, the luggage never arrived. Everyone was sweltering in their woolen sweaters and itchy pants. She borrowed a pair of scissors from a ticket agent and cut off the sleeves, which they used as headbands. She took the scissors to their pants, made makeshift shorts and hailed a taxi.

As this disheveled family of five crowded into a cab, the driver had a good laugh at their outfits. It turns out he spoke English and asked what happened. Against her normally private nature, she told him. He invited her family to his home and she said yes. Clearly she needed help and couldn't rely on herself anymore.

For the next two weeks, her family did not shop. They did not tour museums. They did not eat at restaurants.

They ate home-cooked meals around a plain wooden table with the taxi driver's wife, her sisters, their kids and 20 other people with names she could barely pronounce on Day 1. But by Day 20, she knew them as well as her own family's names.

The kids ran around barefoot with 21 children who didn't speak their language but sure knew how to laugh.

Her husband helped re-upholster the taxi driver's car, which earned the family some extra money, which they turned around and used for a goodbye feast when the time came to finally fly back home.

With bellies full of food and hearts full of gratitude, they said their tearful goodbyes and boarded the plane. As they flew back, the mother couldn't help but think that Africa was a far cry from England. It wasn't as civilized. It wasn't as comfortable. But it was exotic. It was different. And her family bonded more in that two-week unplanned adventure in an African village than they ever would have in a pristine London hotel.

That mama, despite feeling like she would drown in despair, faked a good attitude until a true, authentic joy bubbled up from the pit of her soul. Despite not signing up for it, she made the best of the situation and had an adventure of a lifetime.

You will, too. Grab your T.S. passport. T.S. is an adventure. It might seem scary, but let this book be your road map.

Let me be your tour guide. Let my story serve to remind you that you're not the first to take this scary trip. It's going to be a bumpy ride, but I promise you'll land safely with your child intact.

Buckle your seatbelt. It's time to Happily Tick Off.

Chapter 1
UnrealisTIC

"Have no fear of perfection. You'll never reach it."
~ Salvador Dali

I'm not the first parent in the world to feel insecure about parenting, nor will I be the last. Special needs or not, giving birth is one big lottery ticket. You are literally making a bargain with the universe that you will do everything in your power to keep your kid safe, to make him strong, to give him values and a sense of self, but at any time he could come down with some devastating illness or get hit by a taco truck. And just like that, all those years of telling him to pick up his socks or shut the fridge to save five cents would be wasted. And you'd never be able to eat Mexican food again.

The above statement sounds so fatalistic. Most people prefer not to even think about it, and who can blame them? It's scary. It's unnerving. And it's exactly these terrifying fears that drive today's marketing.

Rich ad execs everywhere are mortgaging their mansions based on Just In Case advertising: Bank that cord blood *just in case* your kid comes down with some terminal illness . . . Spend the extra hundred and fifty dollars on the Britax car seat *just in case* you're hit by an out of control taco truck . . . Buy the brand name diaper cream *just in case* your baby's butt breaks out in hives and ruins your Disney Cruise. For that matter, book that Disney Cruise whether or not you can afford it *just in case* your kid grows up to hate you. You can show him, and the grandkids, those pictures of the four of you in Mickey hats coughing up a lung with laughter on the lido deck. Now how could you be a bad parent with proof like that?

Like most people, I wanted the best for my toddler. While I prided myself in not falling prey to every Mommy and Me Groupon that promised to make my son smarter than Einstein, I was also on a pretty strict budget. I couldn't afford a four hundred dollar car seat or a fancy vacation even if I wanted one. But I did want the best for his education.

As the product of Catholic school myself, I was sure my son would enjoy the same benefits of a private Christian environment – and it was never too early to start. Nicky was three – a year away from his Tourette's diagnosis. As far as I was concerned, his educational career would be nothing but smooth sailing, so why not start him off right?

Against my husband's wishes on the matter, who figured the local community college co-op would be just fine for our active and friendly tyke, I signed Nicky up for an elite preschool ten miles away. Distance was no barrier to my son's learning. He deserved the best. And that "best" just happened to reside on a campus adjacent to the very grammar school I had attended.

The day I turned in his registration – an intense intake form that was more detailed than his hospital exit papers – I ran into women I hadn't seen in twenty years. Those freckle-faced schoolgirls of my memories had morphed into botoxed thirty-something women. Ugg boots replaced saddle shoes. Flat ironed hair replaced ponytails and braids. The only thing familiar was the uneasy pit in my stomach.

I don't belong here, I thought to myself. *Why am I traveling so far just to send my kid to preschool?*

"Andrea *Frazer*??!" I looked across the room to find a lithe tanned woman waving at me.

"Jenny LaGuardia?" I responded. There was no

mistaking that lilt in her voice or that flashing smile. She came over and gave me a big hug. "It's Jenny McQuillan now. Mother of three...almost *four*." She placed her hands over her burgeoning stomach in an "Oops we did it again" smirk.

"A knocked-up Barbie" crossed my brain, but out of my lips came, "You look beautiful!"

She looked me up and down, eyeballs popping, "You're still so tall!"

I thought to respond, "Powerful insight, Captain Obvious," but instead went with, "Thank you!" My answer really made no sense. Nor did this discomfort over a woman I hadn't talked to in two decades. But there it was, insecurity hanging like incense from a May Procession.

This time, instead of fainting from the fumes at the altar, I fumbled a classy exit retort, "Well, I better go retrieve my son. That's him over there, rabidly licking the condensation off the Sparklett's water bottle."

A different woman might have torn up those registration papers, grabbed her son, and made a beeline for the closest exit, but not me. I had a dream – one that included my son playing side-by-side with the offspring of people *I* played side-by-side with. The fact that, as a child, I didn't play side by side with these folks so much as sit on the sidelines and watch *them* have a grandiose time didn't faze me. I was older now and so were they. New bonds would form. New memories would blossom. We were older, more spiritually mature, guided by Montessori and Jesus and *Damnit to Betsy* it was all going to work.

On my way out I glanced at the fresh white walls. Above the lobby couch hung photographs of the happy shiny children of the Vatican. Black hands intertwined with white hands. Asian eyes danced among Irish and Italian. Various colors served as frames around the children, but no worries: the photos hung in perfect symmetry, left to right, up and down. If I had a ruler, I was positive that the space between each photo, at every angle, would measure the exact same number of inches.

And what a relief, really. Isn't such balanced symmetry what the high tuition was for? There could be silliness and laughter and outright joy, but for heaven's sake, let's keep it orderly, shall we?

I wasn't smug enough to believe I could control my son's destiny as precisely as a puppeteer controls a marionette, but I felt an immense amount of pride at the seeds I was planting for his future.

Like many mothers with hopes and dreams for her child, I had mine. I pictured him progressing seamlessly from one milestone to the next: first day of kindergarten with skinned knees under crisp uniform shorts . . . second grade First Communion in a black suit with a toothless grin . . . third and fourth grade chorus (or maybe even a lead . . . HOW EXCITING!) in the school plays.

My fantasies never included my lanky son wearing a basketball uniform or kicking his way into soccer stardom, but that's because neither my husband nor myself are athletes. The closest this kid was going to get to a good arm was angling the Wii remote at just the right angle or perhaps pushing an overstuffed Costco cart through a crowded warehouse.

Regardless of what Nicky excelled in extracurricular-wise, I knew for certain that one prime attribute would punctuate his academic career, and that fine little character trait was nothing other than good old fashioned order. For a while, my little fantasy was indulged. Nicky had friends. Nicky had play dates. Nicky had party invites. But, as the old adage goes, all good things must come to an end. I just didn't expect that ending to begin when he was only four.

It seemed like just another sunny day in beautiful Los Angeles. I was in my son's classroom, gathering up his things for an after school park day, when his preschool teacher stopped me.

"Mrs. Frazer," she said, "I need to talk to you about something I've been observing in Nicky the past few weeks."

I was expecting her to say something like, "Nicky's really getting his letters down" or maybe something a bit less complimentary like, "Nicky needs to work on sharing a bit more." Instead I heard, "I've noticed Nicky stimming on the carpet."

"He's doing what?" I asked, now alarmed. From the tone of her voice, she was far from being critical, but she was clearly concerned. For someone with a dream co-dependently tied to my son's success, "concern" from her translated into "blood-draining-from-my-face toxic fear" for me.

As I waited for her response, I tried to look normal. Since that meant not hyperventilating and passing out against the Lego station, I sucked in my breath and forced myself to look her in the eye.

"By stimming, I just meant he's been rocking back and forth on the carpet during circle time the past few weeks," she replied.

"Oh," I tried not to overreact, "And . . . that's distracting for the other kids?"

"Not at all!" She smiled. "It's just that, well, he's never done that before . . . which is why I didn't say anything at first, but since it's been a bit of a pattern, I thought you'd want to know."

"Well of course I want to know. But, um, for lack of sounding obtuse, why do you want me to know?"

"I suppose because it could indicate something else is going on. And really, I'm not trying to say there *is* anything going on, but sometimes kids who self-soothe are doing it because they are anxious or stressed because there is indeed something else going on. Again, I don't *know,* but I thought *you* would want to know."

As much as I was enjoying this round-and-round, I decided to save it for ring around the rosy later that evening with his younger sister. For the time being, I had about all I could take, bid a hasty thanks and went to the park as planned.

Okay, who am I kidding? I got into the car, called my mother, called my husband, called my best friend and made a bee-line for home where I hastily looked up every possible reason for stimming that could possibly exist. The results were not encouraging. In a nutshell:

Self-stimulatory behavior, also known as **stimming** *and self-stimulation, is the repetition of physical movements, sounds, or repetitive movement of objects common in individuals with developmental disabilities, but most prevalent in people with autistic spectrum disorders.*

A good friend of mine was wise, and kind enough, to remind me not to jump to any conclusions. If I hadn't seen this behavior in my son at home, why should I freak out over one observation from a preschool teacher? Maybe he had gas, or was just a little excited from too many sugar cookies at the holiday party.

As it turned out, Nicky stopped rocking back and forth on the carpet soon after that first meeting. Instead, however, he replaced it with other odd behaviors. For a while, he would clear his throat a few times a minute. If it hadn't been for the teacher's first observation, I might not have noticed it at all. But now, I was watching him like a hawk and it was hard to ignore. I chalked it up to allergies, because eventually his throat clearings disappeared. I prayed the decongestant I gave him was the answer and was grateful for the respite.

But it didn't last long.

After a month of relative quiet, he began darting his eyes back and forth. After administering Benadryl, they went away within a week. Yes, it must be seasonal allergies. What a relief.

But then the head bobs came in. Whenever he was lost in concentration – on a Scooby Doo cartoon, or simply grabbing paper from a printer – jerk-jerk-jerk would go his little head. Grasping at straws, I gave him some more Benadryl, but this time, the nods didn't go away.

One night, sitting around the table, he began playing with a cd player. Every time he'd press the button, the music would pour out, along with a head nod. When he'd press the stop button, his head would nod again.

"Nicky?" I asked him tentatively, "I noticed that you're kind of jerking your head up and down a lot. I'm wondering, if you don't mind telling me, why you do that?"

He was so engrossed, he didn't even look up from his task at hand. Non-chalantly he answered, "Oh, that's easy, Mama. You see, it's kind of like someone has a remote control. But it's not like Papa's remote. It's invisible. And he keeps pointing it at my head. I can't help it."

A few days later, as if in some conspiracy to bang me over the noggin with clarity, I happened to be flipping channels on the TV when Oprah came on. During this particular episode, a man by the name of Brad Cohen was being interviewed. He had just been honored with the prestigious "Teacher of the Year" award.

What made his story so compelling was not only the powerful effect he had on his students, but that he also had severe Tourette Syndrome. His vocal and physical tics were of epic proportion. He admitted that it wasn't an easy road, but he was grateful for them because they taught him empathy and understanding for all people. It taught his students to focus on the human, not the outer shell.

Nodding my head, not unlike my child, I flipped off the TV. I knew two things without a shadow of a doubt then:

1. My son had Tourette Syndrome.
2. I was in trouble.

Takeways & Tips

- Choose an educational environment that is best for your child, not for you.

- Stay open-minded to what your child's teacher has to say. Often it takes someone objective to show us what we don't see.

- Consider finding another mom who's traveled down the same path as you. If you can't find one when it comes to tics, find one that has dealt with a syndrome on the spectrum. While your child might not have autism, per say, there's a decent chance that mother has had a similar emotional journey to you.

- If at first you're distraught over tics and need a break, take a break! Hand your child off to your spouse. No spouse around? Find a neighbor. Find a relative. Consider tics an opportunity to push out of your comfort zone and create some community for yourself.

- It's okay to have sad feelings. Cry. Let it out! The quicker you do that, the quicker you can concentrate on your task at hand: a plan for your child.

- Don't watch TV shows or anything about Tourette's that puts you in fear mode. (Heck, put down this book if you need to. But I promise, it's way more hopeful than a downer.)
- Know that you are not alone – you are going to be okay!

Chapter 2
CinemaTIC

"The whole of life is just like watching a film. Only it's as though you always get in ten minutes after the big picture has started, and no-one will tell you the plot, so you have to work it out all yourself from the clues." ~ Terry Pratchett, Moving Pictures

Selling a movie isn't much different than being handed a Tourette's diagnosis. Both involve stories of heartfelt love, drama and unpredictability. Most people have a general idea of what might be involved to proceed, but when push comes to shove, no one is really prepared for all the twists and turns.

What path does one take?

What people do you need to speak to?

Do you have to spend a ton of time and money to get great results, or is it just one giant crap shoot? And really, like the script itself, is there a happy ending?

It occurs to me that despite big talk about loving the adventure of movies and parenthood, everyone feels the most safe and satisfied when they can count on the big shiny finale. Give us happy bows and Happy Meals. Let us get fat on security and hold a bit tighter to our overpriced gallon-sized Diet Cokes through the scary parts, because at the end it'll be worth it. That theme song will blare and the credits will roll. Boy that was sure scary there for a while, but look how great it all turned out. And that heroine sure had great hair the entire time – even during the knife fight.

The problem with tics is that you can't count on that perfect happy ending wrapped up with a bow. There are millions

of ways to manage Tourette's, and with a personal plan, created through trial and error, oftentimes one can suppress the symptoms a good deal . . . but there is no perfect solution.

With this syndrome, you can't sit back, like at the movies, and watch the hero make a few mistakes but ultimately gain the shiny prize of happiness in the end. You have to be the hero.

When it comes right down to it, watching the hero and being the hero are two completely different ballgames. Viewing the hero from a comfortable theater seat is encouraging and uplifting. In a cocoon of darkness, you are akin to a child in the womb – enjoying life from in an insulated bubble of safety.

When you're the hero, it's downright terrifying. Despite heart-pounding anxiety and fear of failure, you have to forge a new path to a new land – not just for you, but for the well-being of your entire family.

You don't get to be inspired. You have to be inspiring.

You don't get handed the happy ending. You have to earn it.

When Nicky got his diagnosis at age four, I wasn't ready to be a hero. I wanted a hero to save me. I would gladly enjoy an action adventure, but I wanted to watch it, not live it. Where was the caped crusader when a gal needed him? The movie could have been so awesome. I watched it so many times in my head those first few months, I memorized the script.

THE ADVENTURE MOVIE
The Tic Wrangler Rides Again

THE SETTING: BEDROOM.

It's night.

A YOUNG MOTHER reads by the light of the moon at her

bedroom window. Tears of frustration spatter onto her 2000-page self-help book.

Close up of book title: *The Incurable Curse of Tourette Syndrome, its Psychopaths, and its X?!#! X?!#! X?!#! Cursing Component.*

She looks up from the page and her eyes widen like a middle-age pant size. Standing in her bedroom window is none other than the handsome rugged hero she's been longing for—The Tic Wrangler!

With strong jaw line, long legs and a five o'clock shadow, he looks exactly like her husband, only he's wearing cowboy boots and has a cartridge belt filled with silver bullets slung round his hips.

He leans against the doorjamb with his white Stetson cocked at the perfect angle.

She drops her book to the floor. "Be still my beating heart," she whispers in a Scarlett O'Hara accent. There's a new sheriff in town, and he's not leaving to fix his car or watch *Modern Marvels: The History of the Cheese Wheel.* Those gray-green eyes are looking at her—through her—and he understands it all.

The Tic Wrangler: Sounds like you ran into some twitch trouble, little lady.

Mother: Oh, I have! Those darn nasty tics . . . I just can't fight 'em!

The Tic Wrangler flexes his bulging muscles, and the silver bullets glint like stars in the warm summer light.

The Tic Wrangler: Why's a pretty little lady like you taking on such villains all by your lonesome? It would be my honor to fight those pesky T.S. varmints for you.

Mother: Oh, Tic Wrangler, you would do that for me?

The Tic Wrangler: Yes, and I won't even beg for sex.

Mother: (Heavy sigh.) You really are my hero!

The Tic Wrangler: This town ain't big enough for our family and those tics. High noon, it'll all be over.

He sweeps her up in his arms. For the first time since her son's diagnosis, she feels safe. Someone besides her is in control.

Mother: Where are we going?

The Tic Wrangler: Into the sunset, my dear.

Mother: Oh, Tic Wrangler! Is there anything you can't do?

The Tic Wrangler: Laundry.

Mother: Fair enough. Call that horse of yours!

A beautiful white horse appears majestically at her window. The Tic Wrangler jumps onto it, then lifts the mother in his strong arms and places her in front of him. She rests her head against his muscle-bound chest and takes in his scent of leather and Musk.

Mother: All feels right, finally!

Tic Wrangler: Like the gorgeous view, the sun is setting on your little tic problem.

As they ride into the sunset, the clouds form the words: *Tourette's Cured.*

Cue Theme Music. Words slowly scroll across the screen: And they all lived happily ever after, Tic and Fancy Free.

The End.

Fade Out.

The above script might appear slightly exaggerated. After all, as much as I wanted the T.S. to vanish, I didn't really expect a superhero to hitch his horse to my mailbox and fix everything. But the reality of a syndrome that had no answers felt equally far-fetched.

Having lived thirty-five years where no ailment of the

body couldn't be fixed by a prescription, and no ailment of the heart couldn't be soothed by friends, family and the balm of time, I was completely unprepared for the life script I was handed. The theme felt dark. The characters felt rigid and boring. The plot felt dismal. What producer in his right mind would finance a film like this?

Perhaps if Nicky's diagnosis were presented to me as a French film, complete with English subtitles, I'd ease into the experience more easily.

THE FOREIGN FILM

THE SETTING: NEUROLOGIST'S OFFICE

The location is a cross between a doctor's exam room and a chic French café. A young MOTHER, dressed in a designer outfit and heels, sips cappuccino at a red-checkered café table. Candles replace overhead lights.

There are canisters of cotton balls and stirring sticks, along with cookies and coffee grinds. An exam table is present, where her YOUNG SON lays in a vintage coat, wool shorts and cap. His chubby legs sport fat feet, which are tucked into leather walking shoes. He is so friggin' cherubic the mother could eat him, but she sticks to her bread and olive oil instead.

The son is being examined by a HANDSOME DOCTOR who wears a white lab coat and a beret on his head.

ENTER SOUND EFFECTS: Soothing French music

The doctor, after winking at the young boy and handing him a bright yellow balloon, turns to the mother.

Doctor: Beautiful Madame, no worries. It's a small case of zee tics. Have some Chianti, switch to gluten free baguettes and enjoy your life.

Fade out.

Yeah, right.

Instead, this was my experience:

THE DOCUMENTARY

SETTING: NEUROLOGIST'S OFFICE

Glaring overhead lights shine down on smudged white walls and grey linoleum. A YOUNG MOTHER sits on a plastic chair with a TWO-YEAR-OLD GIRL (EVIE) on her lap singing the alphabet song. A curly topped FOUR-YEAR-OLD BOY (NICKY) bounces a white balloon made from a doctor's plastic glove.

A DOCTOR, dressed in a white lab coat, turns to the mother. She does not smile.

Doctor: Your son has Tourette Syndrome.

Mother: (Shaken) But . . . wow . . . really? You've only seen him for five minutes.

Doctor: True. But based on the information you gave me—that he's been making slight vocal sounds and movements for over one year—he has it.

Mother: Okay, then. What now?

Doctor: You can consider medication. Or you can just wait it out. Some kids don't need it and just live with the condition. (Looks at boy.) It doesn't seem to bother him.

Mother: Not now. But what about later?

Doctor: Well, that's where the "wait it out" part comes in.

Mother: What about the whole cursing part of Tourette's?

Doctor: Coprolalia. Yes, that's an unfortunate component for some kids. But less than ten percent get that.

Mother: So the chances of my son getting that?

Doctor: Well, you have a ninety percent chance of avoiding it.

Mother: ~~You are a jerk. I hope if you ever have a child you get assigned a doctor just like you who tells you that instead of a nose your child has grown a honking elephant trunk.~~ What about progression of symptoms?

The doctor stares at her. She does not blink. Clearly she does not have Tourette's. Good for her!

Mother: Since he was diagnosed so young, will it get worse, or do you think it might remain the same or even get better?

Doctor: Hard to say. It could get better. It could get worse. We'll have to wait and see.

Mother: What about his social life? Will he have behavior problems or trouble making friends?

The doctor looks at the boy who is sucking on three of the five fingers of the blown up glove, making his sister giggle.

Doctor: It depends on the child. You'll have to wait and see.

Mother: So you're telling me, after giving my boy nothing more than a five-minute physical exam, that my son has some major neurological disorder that may or may not get worse? It may or may not impede his social and emotional growth? It may or may not warrant heavy narcotics, depending on twists of fate, his own brain chemistry, or some combo of the two?

Doctor: That's correct. Would you like a follow-up appointment in six months?

The mother glares at the doctor.

Mother: I suppose I'll have to wait and see.

Fade out.

After hearing the above scenario the first time, a friend of mine asked if perhaps I portrayed the doctor too broadly. "Is it possible," she prodded, "That in your grief over the unexpected diagnosis, you perceived the neurologist as harsher than she actually was?"

I took a moment to think about it. I wish she were right, but the truth of that visit was as cold and flat as the neurologist's bedside manner. "No. That woman needed a class in Empathy 101."

Turns out the nutritionist we saw next needed a class in Stupidity 102.

THE MEDICAL DRAMA

SETTING: DOWNTOWN HOSPITAL HALLWAY

A MOTHER pushes a YOUNG TODDLER GIRL in a stroller. Her FOUR-YEAR-OLD SON walks beside her down a dated corridor. After jumping from one speckled vinyl square to another, he hangs around his mother's legs.

Boy: Mama, why did we have to drive so far to come here?

Mother: Because we don't have a food expert at our local doctor's building.

Boy: How come?

Mother: Because we have an HMO.

Boy: What's that?

Mother: It's medical language for cheap-butt insurance.

Boy: That sounds awful.

Mother: It is. But we need it to help us when we're sick.

Boy: But I'm not sick, Mama.

She hugs him. Then he clears his throat. Once. Twice. Three times a ticker!

CLOSE UP: Boy's eyes. They dart from side to side.

CLOSE UP: Mother's eyes. They're full of love and concern and don't blink.

Mother: Of course you're not sick. Insurance also helps

people who are already healthy and happy.

Boy: Like you and Papa!

The mother's mood darkens as she walks past door after door after door.

Mother: Oh, yes! Even though Mama goes to all these fun appointments alone and eats lunch out of a brown bag while Papa eats with interesting people in restaurants every day who wear fancy suits without stains, Mama is so happy because Papa has a job and makes money! Lots of money! Cold hard cash is fun!

She is now walking faster as the boy runs next to his mother to keep up. The boy starts to giggle.

Boy: Mama is running! I run when I'm happy, too. I also jump.

The boy jumps. The mom, who is punchy, starts jumping too.

Mother: Why not? Jumping is fun. Jumping and running late and pushing secondhand store strollers is fun. And really, who needs new strollers or gym memberships, because it's not stuff that makes someone happy, right?

The boy starts singing. "If you're happy and you know it clap your hands!"

The mother claps also, too loud. The toddler girl starts crying.

Boy: Evie is not happy. Maybe we should go home.

Mother: (Through gritted teeth) No. We came all the way down here to meet an expert who has the answers to everything.

Boy: I thought Papa was the expert who had all the answers.

Mother: Not when it comes to cooking healthy.

They approach a door that reads "Nutritionist."

Mother: Ah, finally. Here we are. This person is going to teach us a whole lot about good food to help our bodies stay even healthier.

Boy: She sounds really smart.

Mother: She's beyond smart. I can't wait for you to meet her.

Smash cut to:

SETTING: NUTRITIONIST'S OFFICE

A bumbling woman with a thick accent reads a chart.

Nutritionist: Your son has... how you say... Torest?

Mother: Tourette's.

Nutritionist: I never heard of it.

Mother: (Dumbfounded.) How can that be?

Nutritionist: Mam... Mam... we treat so many people. Is impossible for us to know about every condition out there.

The mother's eyes sting from threatening tears. The toddler is still crying. The boy, who has been playing with a blow up doctor's glove, pops his balloon. Now he's crying.

Nutritionist: Oh, no, da pity! Da pity!

She hands the boy a lollipop and the mother a tissue.

Mother: (To boy) Oh, sweetie, you shouldn't eat that.

The boy starts crying harder.

Nutritionist: Oh, can he not have sugar? Da pity!

Mother: It's not just the sugar. I hear the food dyes can interfere with brain synapses, triggering tics.

Nutritionist: Everything in moderation, Mam. It's fine. Besides, he tic. So vat? He no have cancer. He be fine.

The boy grabs the lollipop and stops crying. The toddler, who now has a sippy cup, stops crying. The mother blows her nose and tries to stop crying.

Mother: I'm sorry. I just drove all the way out here in traffic . . . and I'm tired . . . and . . .

The boy starts coughing.

Nutritionist: And your son has a cold on top of it.

Mother: Not exactly. It's part of . . . oh never mind. (She takes a deep breath.) Look, maybe if you can't help me with Tourette's specifically, you can tell me your thoughts about food-related tics. I've done a lot of research on the internet and I've heard going gluten-free can really help. What do you think?

Nutritionist: I think you need be careful about trusting everything you read online. It not like many these people are experts or anything.

The mother's jaw drops. The daughter's sippy cup drops. The boy's lollipop drops. The children scream.

Fade out.

Over the next few months, there were many rewrites to the above scripts. Often they consisted of changes of scenery. Instead of optometrist or neurologist offices, I'd find myself in Urgent Cares or emergency rooms due to face scrunches so severe I was sure Nicky was having a seizure.

"There's nothing out of the ordinary," the doctors would tell me, pulling him out of an MRI machine.

"That was better than the Star Tours ride at Disneyland!" my son would proclaim, despite lying still for thirty minutes straight while I told him stories of Scooby Doo and the Spooky Tunnel of Light.

From blood work to EKGs, I did everything in my power to find a reason for my son's condition, but in the end found nothing but clean bills of health. I was happy he wasn't dying of a brain tumor, but frustrated there were no concrete answers.

Perhaps a more rational person would stop fighting at some point. But at the beginning of my son's diagnosis, I was far from rational. This was my baby, and in my gut, it didn't make sense that there wasn't relief out there. Nothing my husband or friends could tell me about "acceptance" would do.

Perhaps no cowboy was going to take me away to Twitch-Free Country, but I wanted answers. Nothing but complete annihilation of those tics would do. Tourette's was my nemesis and I was John Wayne. I wanted a silver bullet.

One year later . . .

With the tics still waxing and waning with no obvious pattern, the one predictable piece of his future was his education. At least he'd be going to school with his buddies from preschool.

Oh, wait, he wouldn't be.

While all my friends' kids received formal welcome letters to the grammar school adjacent to the preschool, my son did not. I wondered if this had to do with the fact that I'd been so open about my son's diagnosis. Should I not have said anything to his teacher? Was I too transparent with other moms about my fears? Was this letter a passive-aggressive way of telling me, "We don't want his kind here?"

I was bewildered, hurt, but most of all, angry. After three years of financially supporting the preschool, and getting nothing but glowing reports about my son's educational abilities, I never saw this coming.

Spurred on by fury, I set an appointment for the following day. Rejection letter in hand, I wanted an answer, and they were going to give me one. I sat in the lobby and waited, steam coming out of my ears.

As a do-gooder Catholic schoolgirl, I wasn't used to sitting in the principal's office. Little did I know, this would be the first of many principal meetings, over many years, regarding my son. Experience would make such conferences easier, and a sense of humor would help make a few of them laughable. But that day I was in no mood for a chuckle.

After finally being lead into the principal's office, I was

informed that Nicky didn't grasp his pencil correctly in the interview process.

"You've got to be kidding..." I started to balk, but before I could continue she added, "He seems a bit immature."

After peeling myself off the floor and holding back my urge to scream our Lord's name—and not because there was a lovely oil painting of Christ hanging behind this woman's head—I told her how disappointed I was. "He's five. He's not supposed to be mature. And why does it matter if he can grip a pencil correctly? Isn't this what he's supposed to learn in kindergarten?"

She gave me a fakey-compassionate half-smile. "His lack of coordination is disconcerting. It implies he'll need some special attention that we just can't give when there are thirty kids in the classroom and only one teacher."

To which I responded, "With a ratio like that, why would I want to spend six grand a year on his schooling?"

To which she responded, "For the Christian education."

"Oh, yeah, I can really feel God's love here."

And with nothing but a few cursory closing statements, I walked out of that office, enrolled my son in a public charter school, and have never looked back. It's not as fancy as the private school of my dreams. But behind peeling paint is a structure built on joy that fosters creativity, self-worth and joy beyond my wildest expectations. And guess what: It's FREE. And the student-to-teacher ratio is twenty-four to one. Jesus would be proud.

<u>Takeways & Tips</u>

- Remember that you're not a secondary player in your movie script of life. You are the lead. Make your story exciting.

- Remember, you are a hero! Heroes make mistakes, but they win in the end. What do they win? Character and the envy of others who weren't courageous enough to leap to the challenge. YOU can do this! (PSSSST: Heroes cry. It's okay. But they also laugh like crazy.)
- Don't be surprised if it takes a while to get an appointment with a neurologist.
- Also don't be shocked if said neurologist is not that emotional. To be fair, there are indeed some neuros who know how to emote like the wind! But many are logical and to the point.
- For your own peace of mind, get your child checked out from head to toe to be sure that nothing more serious is going on.
- Ask yourself if you're making medical appointments from a place of fear or a place of logic. If it's fear, take a deep breath and slow down. If it's truly T.S., the symptoms aren't going away any time fast. Treat it as a marathon, not a race. Lace up and prepare for the long haul.
- Consider not telling everyone you meet that your son has T.S.. Most people won't even notice. Find a few trusted comrades you can confide in rather than telling the world.
- If your child isn't accepted into a certain group or school, it's okay to be mad about it. But afterwards, consider being grateful. As someone once told me, "Rejectin is protection." Our kids deserve environments that they can grow in. Plus, pressure brings on tics. Consider a peaceful learning environment over an intense one.

- Speak your mind, but try to be graceful. Yes, your child is the best thing since sliced bread. But the fact is, not everyone likes bread. Stop trying to parent based on others and parent based on YOUR kid.
- Bonus tip: if your child has siblings who aren't ticking, don't forget to pay attention to their needs, too!

Chapter 3
ScholasTIC

"I have never let my schooling interfere with my education." ~ Mark Twain

If you're reading this and you have a super young child, it might be hard to believe that there is life beyond the play-dough station and the worries over who got what teacher for Pre-K. But if you're anything like me, you might also find that a special needs diagnosis has a way of separating life into two categories: crap that matters and crap that doesn't. Having your kid not get a part in the school play because he sings like a dying frog? That's crap that doesn't matter.

But having your kid not succeed socially and academically because you don't want to come clean with his or her educators that he has Tourette's? That's crap that matters.

While there's a time to stay silent about what's going on with your child, there's also a time to speak. For me, it became all about intention. Was I informing a teacher about his condition because I truly wanted what was best for my son, or was I trying to make myself feel better about my insecurities with the disorder? Knowing the distinction made all the difference in the educational decisions I made for him. (This included turning a blind eye to his insistence that he wear Scooby Doo underwear on his head for Crazy Hat Day. I reasoned that a ticker wearing tighty whities on his head with confidence outweighed a non-ticker in no hat who couldn't stand being in her own skin. Hey, wait, I resemble that last remark! Maybe you do, too. I won't judge ya.)

Five Years Later

Fourth grade started out like third grade. It had only been three weeks, and I'd been stopped by the teacher three times. The first incident was innocuous enough.

"Mrs. Frazer!" Nicky's teacher, Mr. Parker, called to me with a we-need-to-talk smile.

I internally kicked myself. *All this could have been avoided if I'd picked him up in the carpool line.* Then I remembered, *just because you avoid an issue doesn't make it go away. It simply prolongs it.*

I had one more thought that went something like, *Stop talking to yourself and pay attention to the teacher—ooooooh, a hummingbird!* At which point I directed my concentration where it belonged. Turns out, if only Nicky had done the same thing, I wouldn't be standing in the blue doorframe of an elementary school room on a Friday afternoon.

"Nicky had a hard time focusing today," Mr. Parker informed me.

Last year, when I heard similar words from his third-grade teacher, my face dropped like a bad L.A. facelift. I was crushed. Four years into his T.S. diagnosis, his tics were still pretty minimal. With his penchant for pink umbrellas and impromptu standup routines, I knew he'd never be an academic soldier, dotting his "i's" and crossing his "t's" with laser precision. But I was still holding on to hope that Nicky's eccentricities wouldn't mark him as *too* different.

Like water resting in two cupped hands, I held tight to my dream that Nicky would skate through grammar school "off the radar." With a nurturing environment and a healthy diet, I'd hoped Nicky would remain the epitome of concentration. He'd be funny, witty and outgoing with his peers and teachers, but he'd know when to pay attention to really exciting things.

Like long division.

And bar graphs.

That's where the water—like my dreams for Nicky's academic life—slipped through my fingers. While it was true he had many friends and was an active and engaged learner, this only applied to people and subjects *he* was interested in. If he found something tedious, his ability to concentrate, like my bank account, was sadly depleted.

Unlike the year before, I now felt more emotionally balanced. Four years and counting makes a makes a mama pretty strong. At six foot one, even if I wasn't having a particularly confident day, I knew how to smile and stand tall. Today's tie-dyed sweats scored from a thrift store for $4.99 were extra bonus reinforcement, and it was time to go in with the big guns.

"You know Nicky has Tourette Syndrome, right?"

There, I threw the bomb.

Instead of exploding words, silence fills the five feet between mother and teacher. I might be a veteran at throwing out the "T.S. Word", but Nicky's teacher is a professional at poker face. He shows neither shock nor smugness.

After waiting a beat, he replies, "I *didn't* know about the Tourette's. But now that you say it, I'm not surprised."

Neither am I. Despite crossing my fingers that others wouldn't notice Nicky's vocal and physical quirks, they had indeed increased over the summer. Call it the chlorine from the pool triggering his throat clears. Call it the two hours a day of Nintendo amping up his excitement, bringing with it a light "ah ah ah" warble that my husband and I lovingly referred to as "The Tarzan." Call it the diet cheats, the staying up late, the camping, the vacationing, the constant stream of friends and family in and out of our home that made quiet time nearly impossible. Whatever I wanted to attribute it to, one thing was certain: my son had Tourette's and there was no hiding it any longer.

"Perhaps I can send you a letter explaining a bit about Nicky's condition," I offer.

"That would be wonderful," he echoes back. His voice is soft and his smile is genuine. I know Nicky is in good hands. Better stated, I know *I* am in good hands. The All-State jingle runs through my mind.

"Let's set up an SST also," he adds.

Aaaah, the SST. I know the drill from last year. Standing for "Student Success Team," the SST is a meeting that takes place between parents, teacher and Vice Principal. Our administrators set these in motion to be sure the needs of each individual student are being met.

After a quick reassurance that "all technicalities are being covered so we can focus on the success of your child," the Vice Principal combs through a checklist that covers, but is by no mean limited to:

- Your child's medical diagnosis
- His home life
- The relational status of the parents
- His after-school activities
- His nutritional habits
- His moods at home
- His moods at Grandma's
- His moods at social events
- And enough additional training to qualify for an interrogation certificate.

In all sincerity, most parents agree that it means the world to have their children in such competent hands. After all, to enroll our babies in this coveted charter in the first place, every single one of us had to put our child's name in a lottery. Only 5% of families with kindergarten kids this particular district are fortunate enough to get picked.

With a rigorous balance of academics and arts, plus gardening and P.E., it's hard for a parent to complain, even about an SST. The SST is not there to shame a child or parent. It is put in place like every other event at the school: to support the child to the best of his ability.

It's simply impossible to walk away from a one-hour conversation that is completely focused on your child—emphasis on the positives first, followed by a game plan to help them succeed—without feeling your offspring has indeed landed in a unique and magical oasis known as the Los Angeles charter school.

That all said, the mere suggestion of an SST has most parents dashing their heads against the sticky dashboard of their SUVs, bemoaning this glitch in their child's once flawless academic career.

I was no exception to this dejection dance. Despite feeling gratitude for Nicky's incredible educators, I was drowning in visions of my attention-deficit class clown ticking like a bobble head on the short bus.

"An SST sounds like a great plan," I smile back at Mr. Parker. With his striped Vans and flat ironed hair, I feel like I'm getting advice from a boy band member.

Given that Mr. Parker has a decade of experience teaching fourth grade, however, and I have zero, I yield to his proposal. "I'll send you my availability along with a little info on Nicky's personality to help you see how he ticks. *No pun intended.*" I wink at my little quip.

He laughs out loud. His guard is down now, which is the best I can hope for in having some honest dialogue this year.

We say our goodbyes and I head toward the lunch tables, where I will no doubt find Nicky hunched over some kid's shoulder—likely a kid he doesn't know—to catch a glimpse of his Mario game. Being a nine-year-old extrovert, some might call Nicky clueless. But most just call him friendly. It's hard not to like a kid who is comfortable enough with himself to not give a rat's arse if you want him sticking his nose in your game or not. His actions imply, "Look, I'm here. I'm not going away. You're the one with the issue if you don't like meeting new people." It's lovely living in Nicky's world.

True to form, Nicky is at the lunch tables. Only this time, instead of hanging over some twelve-year-old's shoulder watching him play, he is seated amiably next to him on the painted green bench. He isn't watching the game, but instead is holding it in his own grimy palms.

In addition to being more social than Facebook, my kid is a con artist.

"Five minutes," I tell Nicky, who responds in a practiced, "*Yeessss*, Mommy." One point for me! My son might not concentrate in class, but he has surely gotten down the routine that you respond to Mom in the affirmative or your distraction is taken away.

On the way to get my daughter, Evie, from her third-grade classroom, I mull over my conversation with Nicky's teacher—how I had made him laugh, and hopefully feel comfortable communicating with me, throughout the fourth grade year. It wasn't so much that I wanted him to like me as a person. I wanted him, as I wanted every teacher every year, to know that I'm a mom who is approachable and willing to take suggestions. I'm a mom who doesn't use my son's "condition" as an excuse for bad behavior. I'm a mom who, of course, thinks my child is more gifted than Santa at Christmas, but I'm also the type to nip precociousness in the bud. Yes, call me the patron saint of accountability, consistency and communication.

And defensiveness.

Because, as much as I hate to admit it, I sometimes go a bit overboard with the whole "He has Tourette's" proclamation. It's as if, in protecting my son, I am telling the world, "I know about Nicky's tics and his ADHD symptoms. You don't have to blast me with your oh-so-clever newsflash on my son's inadequacies. I will shower you with them first, along with a witty joke, because I'm just so okay with this crazy disorder."

Lucky for me, most people were convinced of my security.

Convincing myself was a whole other matter.

Takeways & Tips
• Don't be afraid to listen to your child's educators before making snap decisions that they are all idiots and simply don't understand your wonder kid. (I'm not talking from experience here. *Ahemmmm.*)
• Get real about your child's challenges.
• Get real about your own challenges.
• Honor your child's gifts.
• Honor your own gifts.
• Stop taking everything so seriously. It makes tics more bearable.
• View grammar school as a blip on the radar of your child's life so everything doesn't feel so crushing. In ten years, when they are at Harvard, are you really going to care that some teacher thought your kid was a punk? Stay open and grow!
• Tourette's and education is a marathon, not a sprint. Stretch, be hydrated, and be ready to take this one step at a time. It makes all the difference in the outcome of the race we call parenthood.

Chapter 4
FreneTIC

"But in a home where grief is fresh and patience has long worn thin, making it through another day is often heroic in itself." ~ Melanie Bennett,
Learning to Dance in the Rain

When my son was first diagnosed with Tourette's, my world turned upside down. Instead of appreciating my husband for being the calming anchor in a ship tossed and turned by the waves of my emotions, I wanted to call mutiny. "How dare you be okay when I'm freaking out? Walk the plank and take your friggin' groundedness with you!"

In reality, I never wanted to toss my spouse overboard. All I wanted was for him to throw me a life jacket so I could float from the chaos to the shore of serenity. Little did I know that this was not my husband's job. He could support me the best way he could, but at the end of the day, he was not the captain of tics or captain of me. Only I could charter my course. And you know what sucks the most about that? When my ship began to sink, I had no one to blame but myself. S.O.S.! S.O.S.! Shipwreck taking place! (Psst. Don't panic too much. I survived and you will, too.)

It's seven pm on a Monday night. We're in that magical hour I refer to as the "bedtime routine." Our ten-minute ritual is simple enough and follows a three-pronged model to a successful evening wind down:

- Brush your teeth
- Go pee pee
- Put on pajamas

Followed by twenty minutes of reading and prayers, it's not unrealistic to have lights out in thirty minutes. With the unpleasant prospect of hearing my son throat-clear his way through *Captain Underpants*, however, thirty minutes often morphs into an hour as I distract myself on the internet.

"This won't take long," I murmur to my husband as I quickly scan emails and Facebook updates.

Rex doesn't answer back. I'd love to say he's smiling to himself over this familiar scenario, good-naturedly playing the pragmatic Ricky to my discombobulated Lucy performance.

But I know the truth. He's annoyed that instead of just buckling down and getting these kids in bed, I'm once again allowing my distractions to run the show. Given that my steady-eddy mate goes to bed like clockwork at nine-thirty every evening, regardless of what time the kids finally settle down, my actions are subconsciously ensuring he and I will see even less of each other.

Well, maybe my actions are more conscious than I care to admit.

I'm annoyed with my husband. The tics don't bother him at all. I should be relieved that one of us remains anchored amidst a sea of neurological uncertainty, and yet I'm not. I'm flabbergasted. And frustrated. I don't get how he can stay calm when our son keeps head-nodding over his math homework. For my husband, shoulder scrunching and lip smacking might as well be in the same category as breathing.

"That's just what Nicky does," he says. "It's no big deal."

I'd love to say that my husband, deep inside, is feeling

mortally wounded from the tics. I'd love to say that he feels so much guilt for contributing to a genetic deck of wonky cards that he can't acknowledge the tics at all... that he's covering up his shame with silence and a big act of devil-may-care. But there's only one good reason he isn't a basket case over my son's condition.

The tics don't bug him.

And that somber truth bugs the bloody daylights out of me. How can that be? How can my mate stay so composed?

It's as if a super-force-field of nonchalant mojo power has encapsulated him into a bubble, where he remains forever nonplussed.

Lucky for me, my son's tics bounce off of my husband's bubble and nail me right in the gut.

Every. Single. Time.

Every. Single. Tic.

My reaction annoys me about as much as my husband's inability to react in the first place. You'd think by now I'd be used to Nicky's tics. And on days when he doesn't tic at all, or when they're very low, I can honestly say I've embraced his Tourette's. Isn't that noble of me—to accept noises and shakes when they're nonexistent?

Call me Buddha of Invisible Twitches—I can let go of invisible problems.

But when Nicky's noisy companions make their return, I'm thrown into a tailspin. After all I've done to mitigate them, it's as if every shoulder shrug and tongue click is a knife in my side, seeming to scream to the world, "You failed as a mother! You could not cure your son!"

My husband, sitting there in his plaid Ward Cleaver pajamas, complete with green bathrobe, is the picture of calm acceptance. Up until recently we had many conversations about Nicky's tics. They went something like this:

Me: "He's doing those noises. Do you think it's the granola bar we gave him?"

Him: "I think it's the waxing and waning of the tics, sweetie."

Me: "But we got the organic bars and he's not sick. So why would he start coughing now?"

Him: "Because he has Tourette's."

Me: "But we've done so much to keep him healthy and give him eleven hours of sleep every day. Why would those tics come back?"

Him: "Because he has Tourette's."

Me: "HOW CAN YOU BE SO CALM ABOUT THIS?????"

Him: "Because I know he has Tourette's."

Picture me gazing into his eyes just like on our wedding day. Except instead of beaming with love, I'm sending savage glares that would transform the average man into a quivering pile of mush. My husband, however, is a 1950's cowboy. Elegant, tough, and stubborn as a purebred mule, an angry six-foot wife won't intimidate him. He responds to my anger the same way he does to tics: like it's nothing out-of-the-ordinary.

Him: "He's not going to die from this syndrome, Andrea."

Me: "But those sounds could cause him to miss out socially."

Him: "The gaggle of kids in and out of our house kills that theory."

Me: "I just don't want him teased. I don't want him bullied for tics. I want him to be loved for all his amazing qualities."

Him: "Then love him, because he's awesome. He's not going to miss out on any life opportunities. He just makes a few noises sometimes."

Me: "I know you're right. Of course you're right. He's

going to have good days and bad days, and all we can do is the best we can. It's going to be like the life-bucket theory, right?"

Him: "Right. We keep filling him up with good stuff. That way, when the bad stuff creeps in, the good stuff will outweigh it and we know we'll have done all we can."

Me: "Okay. You're right. I'm just going to accept the fact that he has Tourette's and not stress you out anymore."

Him: "That would be great, honey. I'm proud of you."

Me: "Me too. But just in case, don't give that kid any more granola bars."

And now we're back in the circle. For a guy that can't boogie, Rex has certainly danced around with me for years.

Now, however, we're on opposite ends of the dance floor. Like kids at a high school social, we want to sway with each other in unison, but it's less painful if we stand sulking in our own corners.

"Nicky won't give back Strawberry Baby!" I hear his younger sister, Evie, yell from the upstairs banister.

It's as good a time as any to face the bedtime music. I get up from my computer and take a deep breath.

On my way to the stairs, I glance at Rex.

"I'll go as fast as I can," I mutter on my way up the stairs.

"Love you."

He means it. I just don't feel it. It's not totally his fault, either. I'm done crying over my son's diagnosis. I'm done living in the fear of "What if his condition gets worse?" I'm done wondering if some magic cure exists that, if I only gave myself five more minutes of research time on the internet, I could find the pieces to this confusing puzzle.

If my husband has an invisible shield that keeps him from being annoyed at tics, I've developed an emotional force field. I'm not saying it's healthy, but it keeps me from sucking my thumb in a fetal position in the geranium bushes out front.

As I head up the stairs, I can see the miniature bulbs of Rex's handmade cube light up. Comprised of seven inch by seven inch metal squares, stacking seven levels high, Rex created this rectangular box to program various L.E.D. light displays. The lights are a dazzling emerald. Every evening after work, Rex sits in his armchair and creates new displays. "This one is the Pac Man theme," he'll announce. Or, "Here's the checkerboard pattern from my favorite grammar school video game, Pong!"

"That's awesome!" I often smile back. And it is. Why shouldn't he have something he likes to do? Better stated, he loves it . . . so much so that if I were the jealous type I'd refer to it as his mistress.

My husband would never cheat on me in real life, however, given that he can't multitask. Instead, I've nicknamed his little project "Elphaba" in honor of the misunderstood green witch in my favorite musical, *Wicked*.

The folks in Oz didn't understand Elphaba, so they detached from her. I don't understand my husband's ability to accept the tics, so I'm detaching from his point of view.

No one in the world has a cure for Tourette's, but I can't detach from that. I'm left with two choices:

- I could come to terms with my son's condition. Like Elphaba, I could rise above the confusion and simply, as they say in the act break song, *Defy Gravity*. I could be free.

- I could go round and round in my overloaded brain, trying everything, natural or gimmick-related, to fix my son. Like Elphaba, who thinks she will have peace when she finally meets the wizard, I can keep driving toward an invisible cure.

My head screams, "Choose Door Number One! It's the

only way to win the prize of serenity!"

But my heart whispers, "Choose Door Number Two! It's a long shot, but you'll only be truly happy when your son is free of this maddening curse."

As I open the door to my son's bedroom, I know I will continue to knock down Door Number Two. This will cause me to be forever unhappy. And while logically, I know I can't stop my son's tics, I can't stop trying.

As I wrap my arms around my little guy, I attempt to ignore the throat clears every thirty seconds. I try to remind myself that my son has Tourette Syndrome, not a death sentence. I try to fix my thoughts on the fact that my fourth grader reads at an eighth grade level.

Nicky is joyful, open, loving, generous, funny and kind.

Too bad his mother is crazy. Because as much as she doesn't want to, she'll keep banging her head against Door Number Two. Four years of doing this can hurt the toughest of skulls.

"What's wrong, Mama?" Nicky, ever empathetic, notices I'm not quite up on my game tonight.

I tell him the same thing I'm going to tell Rex later that evening. "I have a headache."

Takeways & Tips

- Don't be surprised if your spouse doesn't have the same emotional reaction to the tics that you do.
- Anger and resentment are common reactions to a difference of opinion in marriage, but don't live there. Kids feel the stress. Stress adds to tics. Want less tics? Be kinder to yourself and your spouse.
- Lest you think the above statement is incriminating you when it comes to tic control, let me also state that you don't have that much power. Your kid might tic if his parents were Prince Charming and Cinderella. Wiring is wiring.
- Lest you think I am telling you that you have no power at all in suppressing tics, I am not saying that. Read on and I'll tell you about a lot I did to help minimize the tics. But guess what? I didn't cure T.S. And I didn't find any helpful solutions at 10PM on a Tuesday night when I was cranky with my spouse. Chances are you won't either. Take it slow.
- Be patient with the journey. It's more important to raise a ticker from a place of emotional stability than to eradicate all twitches but be a basket case. (Trust me on that one.)
- Don't expect your mate to have the same reaction as you. If he did, it could be worse. (Ever think what would happen if BOTH of you freaked out at every nose grimace? No fun at all.)
- Find something you enjoy in life that doesn't depend on stopping tics. Seriously, you need to try. This was the hardest thing for me. Read more in5.

Chapter 5
LunaTIC

"I wish I could tell you how lonely I am. How cold and harsh it is here. Everywhere there is conflict and unkindness. I think God has forsaken this place. I believe I have seen hell and it's white, it's snow-white." ~ Elizabeth Gaskell, *North and South*

Looking back over this period of my life, I'm certain of only two things. The first is that my emotions over the tics were completely unmanageable. The second is that I was a complete and total egomaniac. I had been making the tics all about me and my feelings about them. In fact, I almost re-titled this chapter NarcissisTIC but I decided to cut myself some slack. After all, if you're reading this book, maybe you're just as worried about T.S. as I was.

Rather than call the wah-wah-wambulance on our sorry butts, I'd like us to give ourselves a break for any time spent over-thinking, over-worrying and over-panicking. I'm not saying this kind of neurosis is healthy, but it happens. After all, it's hard to detach from a condition when the person with the condition was once physically attached to us. I want you to know that I understand the grief and the concern. Been there, done that, flogged myself and survived. You, will, too.

It's eleven pm. I'm tired, but I can't sleep. Like the lights on my husband's cube, my brain races round and round.

I need to write this letter to his teacher, but I really don't want to. Because Nicky is fine.

Except, he isn't. Enter Frustration.

At least I'm fine. Enter Jubilation, followed quickly by its victor, Defeat.

Well, actually, I'm not fine. I'm running on four hours of sleep, I'm developing an anxiety disorder, and I haven't had alone time with my husband in ages—which is ironic given that I just finished up a three year romance column for a major magazine.

Despite my ability to crank out posts three times a week, I can't figure out how to write a simple letter to my son's grammar school teacher about why he rolls his eyes uncontrollably and has the attention span of a gnat.

Standing up, I grab my coffee cup for a welcomed distraction and amble into the kitchen. As I set it down in the microwave and hit the start button, my mind drifts back to the task ahead of me. The circular glass tray holding my mug starts turning round and round. As if in some evil co-dependent conspiracy plan, my brain begins spinning again.

I internally bolster myself. *Andrea, the only way to face this SST is by hitting stuff head on and explaining what exactly Nicky's core issues are. It's no big deal really.*

Of course I'm lying, not unlike my mother when she swears that she never notice's Nicky's tics.

I take a breath. I decide to employ a positive thinking technique I learned during one of my late night searches to cure tics. Apparently there is no magical pill or cure for Tourette Syndrome, but there are loads of cognitive behavior remedies for scattered mothers who can't stop obsessing about vocal and physical jerks. One such method that promised to retrain the mind is called splicing. It entails placing a positive thought right after every negative one to transform unproductive emotions into positive ones.

This all sounds fine and good, but the truth is, say your legs have been cut off. You can put on your Snow White Happy

Hat and chirp, "Gee, I am closer to the ground now. It'll be so much easier to pick up loose change and dwarves!" But the truth of the matter is, you've got stubs where limbs used to be. Your legs, like this fakey-wakey positive thinking, have been spliced to the bone.

I'm punchy on caffeine. Dwarves, Elphaba lights, Yuban coffee, and tics: It's everything I hoped my forties would be. I'm ready to play the "T.S. Is Awesome" game. Let the splicing begin.

SPLICING GAME:

Nicky occasionally makes noises. (Negative Thought). But they are very quiet and not an annoyance to kids around him. (Positive Thought!)

He doesn't have the greatest attention span. (Negative Thought!) But he's at the top of his class academically. (Positive Thought!)

He interrupts and argues a lot. (Negative negative *damn that's annoying* NEGATIVE . . .) But he's got a keen mind and a heart of gold. (Positive positive *oh my sweet little ticker* POSTIVE!)

I take a breath. Splicing, schlicing, this letter isn't about condemning Nicky or justifying him. It's information only. I buck up and resolve to state the facts. I promise myself, above all, I won't get emotional.

The timer beeps on the microwave and across the screen it reads in digital letters, "Enjoy Your Meal!"

Oh, short circuit and die a horrible death, you useless box of radar! There is no 'Enjoy Your Meal' because THERE IS NO JOY THANKS TO T.S. I should throw you in the L.A. River. I hastily grab the mug and slam the door.

Better to take it out on the electronics than the L.A. Unified School District. Looking at the empty space where the tic-tock clock used to be, my anger issues do not escape me.

I add some milk to my mug. I'm almost ready to face the music. But first . . . I decide to think about something happy. Like the past! Maybe if I comb through those memories one more time, I'll find the link to the chain of events that led me to a pretty decent case of talking to myself, all the while avoiding real conversations with my husband and cursing radioactive kitchenware.

From my perch on the couch, I eyeball the photos above the mantel. Clustered in perfect unison, the black and white pictures reveal a slice of life from seven years past. My black haired daughter is only six weeks old, being cradled by my husband like a Kabuki doll football. My son is a year and a half, complete with blond curls and a charming grin.

Reminiscent of the moving pictures in Harry Potter's Hogwart's School of Witchcraft and Wizardry, I half-attempt to see my son's little image dart out of the picture frame and out the door.

Part saint, part Huckleberry Finn, and one hundred percent the impish Puck, Nicky was my dream child. Born six weeks early on New Year's Day, Nicky entered the world wired for happy. Unless he was sick or hungry, this kid rarely cried. He slept soundly and played hard. His laughter was infectious. He radiated joy.

Lest you think I thought he was perfect, I saw his faults. He was stubborn. And naughty. And so very crafty.

And yet, he was *my* stubborn, naughty, crafty little kid. And as a mother, I was already channeling his "faults" into his "gifts." I was convinced that his less-than-lovely character traits would be the very same that would propel him into leadership later in life. They would help him avoid peer pressure. Those kinds of personality flaws I could handle, but last I checked, T.S. wasn't a character defect. It was a condition that had no cure. Not only could I not channel Nicky's tics, I could not channel my grief.

Tears sting my eyes. Soon I begin to sob. I don't want to wake up Rex, so I stuff my head into a pillow and let out muffled wails. It's not unlike how I've been living the past few years, stuffing my feelings inside my chest like the stuffing inside the pillow. On the outside, I passed as seamless and strong. I was a comfort for my kids. I was a soft landing place for my family and friends.

But if you looked closely, there was a hole. The sadness over my son's diagnosis was finally leaking out. And not in a trickle. It was a torrent of long-held-back anguish. Sure, I had cried before, but I had always held on to the hope that maybe I'd find an answer to this maddening disorder. That night on the couch, I cried in what can only be called pure defeat. I had waged a valiant war against Tourette's, but it was time to throw down my guns and go home. I had been shot. I wasn't fatally wounded, but I'd forever walk with a limp. Nothing would fix Nicky and nothing would fix me.

There, alone in my living room, I held a funeral. It was time to say goodbye to the childhood I thought my son would have. Time to bury any ideals I carried with me about a seamlessly easy education experience. Time to light candles. One for his beautiful face that often twisted into nose scrunches. One for the friends he'd likely lose due to behavior problems and uncontrollable impulses. One for the bullies who would torment him for jerks he couldn't control.

The biggest candle was lit for me. It burned my eyes with the sad truth that just when I was feeling like I had this whole T.S. thing down pat, I realized how raw my emotions still were. I looked down at the tear-soaked pillow. It was losing its stuffing and I was losing my mind. I wanted to patch the hole, but T.S. didn't have a cure, and I didn't know how to sew.

"Acceptance is the only way to go," friends would tell me.

I agreed. Serenity is supposed to bring peace, but it didn't for me. That night, I accepted that my Rex and I had to work out a better parenting plan so we weren't always at odds. I accepted that tics were not something I could control with a magic potion, drug, good thoughts or prayer. There was no cure and there was no Tic Wrangler.

I accepted that it was time to switch from coffee to a good glass of red wine. And I accepted that tonight that letter would not get written. Before I could even get off the couch, I fell asleep on the pillow. It was a blessing. I needed my rest. Living with a hole in my body was exhausting.

If only someone had told me I wouldn't feel like this forever.

Oh, someone would! Sooner than I would have expected.

Takeways & Tips

- Sometimes life is tougher than Simon Cowell at a Spice Girls lip sync contest.
- Give yourself permission to have a pity party.
- Know when it's time to sober up from the party and drive home.
- Remember that hope exists even if you don't see it at that moment. (You can close your eyes on the shoreline, but it doesn't eradicate the presence of a vast ocean.)
- Don't expect your spouse to process the way you process.
- Be patient with your spouse and yourself.
- Don't ever make drastic decisions about your life when you feel like crud. Sadness passes.
- Your feelings are not facts. Get dramatic all you want, but there's a decent chance your fears about your kid's life aren't actually going to come true, so relax.
- Drink all you want, but tics don't sound any better the next day with a hangover.

Chapter 6
TherapeuTIC

"Think of your head as an unsafe neighborhood; don't go there alone." ~ Augusten Burroughs, *Dry*

If you're like me, going to therapy feels a bit like defeat. It's like saying to the world, "My life is unmanageable. I need help." That's embarrassing.

Then again, if you're reading this and you're like I was, maybe your life is unmanageable. Maybe you've finally hit upon something you can't control on your own and you need help.

When I decided to get some one-on-one counseling, I forced myself to ignore my shame. Instead, I thought about my son and his first attempts to walk. Did I tell him, "Hey, you're on the floor, stupid crab-walker! Get up and use your God-given legs." Of course not. I held out my arms and gently encouraged him, "You can do it. Just take a few steps. Tomorrow, you'll take a few more, and I'll hold your hand until you can do it on your own."

While I was lucky enough to eventually have decent insurance, I know that not all of you do, but that doesn't mean you're out of luck. A good friend, pastor, rabbi or even an online forum can be a lifesaver. Personally, I'm a big fan of the 12-step support groups. Just Google "Alanon" and you'll likely find many meetings in your area that you can attend. While many people attend Alanon to deal with addicts in their family, there's plenty that go to detach from other difficult people, places and things – and in your case, things just happens to be tics. Alanon can help you manage your emotions around a disorder that constantly changes. It can help you find serenity.

Whatever your venue of choice is, the main thing is to find a group or a person you can feel safe with. If you can't be honest and vulnerable, how can you heal? In my case, this safe person was Sam.

"My husband is colder than a freezer on an iceberg during a snow storm."

My therapist, Sam, looks up from his computer and smiles. "Don't mince words," he says. "I really want to know how you're feeling."

I like Sam. In his black Levis, vintage style sneakers, and button down camp shirt, he reminds me of a drug- free Jimmy Buffet. At fifty-six, with his dancing eyes and graying hair, he somehow manages to look hip without trying too hard. And that's because he doesn't.

Sam is light-hearted about everything. Best of all, he's light-hearted about me. He'll patiently hear me rant for ten minutes on everything from elitist L.A. drivers to the price of genetically modified corn at Safeway. He'll gently nod his head as I recall a bedtime encounter with Nicky when my sensitive son bawled for ten minutes at the thought me of getting into a car crash.

When I get to the part where Nicky cries out in all seriousness, "Mama, I love you so much, if you got dead, I'd make a craft out of you," Sam's somber expression suddenly breaks into a smile as wide as the Texas sky. At that point he starts laughing so hard, I can't help but laugh with him.

Sam doesn't view me as overly emotional or needy. He sees me as human. Granted, I'm paying him by the hour to do so, but I get the impression that he enjoys my company as much as I enjoy his. Either he's a shyster artist who knows just how to react to get me to come every week, or he genuinely cares about my growth. I'm going with the second option. Frankly, even if it's the first, I don't care. My bi-monthly talk sessions grease the wheels of a life that often feels stagnant.

"How are the tics this week?" he asks.

"Not so great. I know it's the nature of the syndrome, but I guess I haven't quite accepted it yet. But I'll be fine." I sigh.

"You don't seem fine," he'll say.

"Well, of course I'm not *really* okay, but it's not like I'm going to die from a few tics. Nicky is happy as a clam. I just wish I could feel better about it. And I don't . . . And that stinks.. . " I fumble with the zipper on my jacket. "I just want things back to the way they were before."

"You mean before the Tourette's?"

"The Tourette's . . . the tension between Rex and me about how to handle them . . . I mean, things used to be really, really good."

"In what way? Tell me about when it was really, really good."

"I can't think back that far. My brain will strain and I could die right here on your 1980's sofa. Or is it a loveseat? You really need some better décor if you want to attract some higher paying crazies."

This time Sam doesn't smile. He looks at me pretty seriously.

"You use humor a lot," he says. "Which is okay. You're pretty funny. But smart people like you often use it to cover up deeper hurt. I want to hear about that hurt. What are you afraid of?" he asks.

"Of *hurting*, jerk wad!" is what I want to say. Instead, I go with, "I guess I'm scared of what I'll uncover."

"That's what therapy is about," he says. "It's like an onion. You peel off layer after layer. Eventually, you find the truth."

"Yeah, well unpeeling an onion sounds like a great analogy, but the more you peel, the more you cry. And eventually, if you keep on peeling, there's nothing but a small little stub where an onion used to be."

"You're afraid of losing yourself,"

"Yeah," I admit.

"You're already lost," he says.

He's right, of course. "Three points for you!" is all I can muster.

"It can only get better from here," he says. "You have to be open and trust the process if you want to feel better."

"Okay," I say. "Let's do this."

I pause before speaking while I attempt to collect my thoughts.

My mind lands on something I read once in some dime store self-help book. It said that peering into the past was like driving forward while looking into the rearview mirror. You're destined to crash.

This adage rings true to me, but in my case, I have to look into the rearview mirror and slowly, every so carefully, reverse. I have to travel back to the life before the Tourette's, before the kids . . . to remember what safety felt like before the giant skin-on-metal collision.

"Ready?" Sam peers at me tentatively. "Tell me about before."

"Okay," I mutter. "Right before I met Rex, I was working in television. I had just landed my first writing gig. For the first time in my life I was making really great money. I had a fabulous walk-up apartment surrounded by trees on one side and a nursery school on the other. Every morning I'd wake up to the sounds of children laughing and go to bed with the sounds of my next-door neighbors having a coffee and chatting on the outside balcony. Life felt rich. I mean, if there was a snapshot of a single girl in her late twenties living the dream, it would have been of me."

"Did you dress as snazzy as you do now?" Sam asks, eyeballing my neon-pink Kangaroo tennis shoes scored from Goodwill just that morning.

"Better. I wore cat eyeglasses with diamonds on the side. My hair was dyed bright red. Oh my gosh – I could actually afford to get it done every other month at a foo-foo salon. And there was nothing in my closet that didn't look good with patent leather Mary Janes. In fact, that was the very ensemble I wore the first night I met Rex."

"And what was your conservative date's response?" Sam inquires.

"He seemed totally unfazed," I answer. "Later, after we'd been dating for a while, I asked him what he had thought. He admitted that he was surprised but intrigued. He said he liked that I was able to be myself."

"Is that true? Did you feel like yourself around him?"

"Totally. He was so calm and easygoing . . . so different from my dad. I loved my father —don't get me wrong—but he was this loud New Yorker who never stopped talking or cracking jokes."

Sam looks at me as if to say, "Gee, I wonder who she got it from," but he gracefully declines comment.

"Growing up, if there was a leak in the sink, we'd have to call a handyman. I swear, my father would stand over that plumber for three hours getting his life story out of him. 'Oh, you're a Catholic like my wife and daughter? Oh, no? You're a member of the Tribe of David like me? Roses are reddish... violets are bluish... if it weren't for Jesus, we'd all be Jewish!'"

Sam busts up laughing. "That's a good one. Your dad sounds like a character."

"Oh, he was. It's just . . . it was sometimes mortifying. If an Asian grocer told him 'Sir, your daughter very beautiful,' he'd make this grand sweeping bow and answer—in a terrible accent, mind you—'Oh, sank you. Her mother Chinese.'"

"So you chose a husband who wouldn't embarrass you, eh?" Sam inquires.

"Yeah," I admit. "It's funny how now the things that drew me to Rex—his quiet demeanor . . . his pragmatism . . . are the things that make me a bit lonely at times."

Sam just stares thoughtfully as I continue. "I guess . . . well . . . I miss the fun my dad brought with him. I think he would have really liked Nicky. They would have understood each other. They both love jokes. They both love people."

"They both had illnesses they had to battle," Sam notes.

Ouch. I wasn't expecting that one. I had told Sam a few sessions earlier about my dad's bipolar condition. I hadn't really made the connection between my childhood fears of my dad's up and down condition and the up and down nature of Nick's tics.

"Um, well, you have a point, Sam," I concede. "But I don't know what any of this has to do with my husband."

"I'm attempting to understand why you don't feel safe now. Clearly you didn't feel 100% safe with your dad's condition, and now you don't feel safe with your husband anymore. Why is that? What went wrong?"

He sees I'm struggling and throws me a bone, "How does the T.S. fit into all this?"

To the outside party, my next statement might seem totally obvious. But to me, it was a new revelation. It hit me like a ton of bricks. "I guess unlike my dad who couldn't fix a sink to save his soul, I chose a man who could fix a gushing fire hydrant with his eyes shut. Rex can build a computer from scratch and remove a car motor. He can fix a TV and a broken lamp and a busted radiator, but he can't fix the tics."

My eyes start to water.

"Here you go," he says, offering me a tissue.

"I'm fine," I say, adjusting my glasses.

"We've been through this already. You're not." he hands me a tissue. I take it.

"Why is it so hard for you to admit you need support?" Sam looks up from his computer where he's been taking notes. His eyes lock with mine. Oh crap, now my eyes are tearing up. I mean, really. Isn't it enough my son is going to turn me into a paper mache' project when I'm a corpse? Now this?

I wipe the tears from my eyes. My voice quivers. "I do ask for support from Rex. But I still feel scared."

"Maybe what you need from him, he just can't give," Sam offers.

On the one hand, this is true. On the other, it's incredibly disappointing. Probably because it puts the ball right back in my court, and it's so much easier to point the blame at my spouse. When I have the ball, I have to do the work. And, well, to quote my kids, "I don't wanna I don't wanna I don't wanna!"

Sam breaks my rumination with one simple question: "Do you know the difference between happiness and joy?"

"No," I admit, blowing my nose like a foghorn.

"Happiness is dependent on outside circumstances. It's dependent on a lot of ifs: 'If' my husband does x y and z to my satisfaction, I'll be happy. 'If' my son stops ticking I'll be happy. Joy is something that one can experience despite less than perfect circumstances."

My ears perk up at that. It sounds good. It sounds real good. But how?

I'm pretty sure that along with his PhD in psychology, Sam has a degree in mind reading, because he adds, "You'll get there. You're strong. You can do this."

And that's when, for the first time in a month, the tiniest

piece of anxiety is lifted from my stomach. In its place is something I haven't felt in quite a while. What was the name of that thing again? Oh, yeah. Hope.

"So let me get this straight. You're saying that even if my son is ticking, I can experience joy. And even if Rex and I disagree on how to handle tics, I can still have joy?"

"Bingo!" he says, throwing up his hands as if to say, "We got this!"

Mentally I threw up my hands also. But instead of tossing them up in despair, I do a small air pump. Maybe some people would get taken down by T.S. and a rough spot of marriage. But it won't to be me. I will be strong. I will be brave. Someone has to be there for my kid. Someone has to keep this marriage on the light and breezy side of the street. Someone has to write a book to help other folks going through this same crazy situation. And someone has to make some good money at some point.

First thing on the list? Donate to the Tourette Syndrome Association.

Second thing? Buy Sam a new sectional. Like my bad attitude, that love seat has to go.

<u>Takeways & Tips</u>
- Finding someone other than your spouse, friends and immediate family is important. You can get an objective opinion and vent.
- Don't go to therapy just to complain. It's okay to get it out, but then listen to what the therapist tells you. That's the key to growth!
- Find a therapist or support group where you feel safe.

- Try to shift your thinking from worrier to warrior.
- Remember – there are no victims, only volunteers. Don't co-sign a life of misery.
- Don't be afraid to cry, scream and generally break down. Sometimes clay vases need to be thrown back in the fire to be resculpted into something beautiful.
- Think of pain as a gateway to growth.
- Consider journaling before you go to therapy so you don't lose sight of your goals in a cloud of emotion.
- Ask your therapist to give you homework every week to work on.
- Don't berate yourself for seeking help. It's actually the best thing you can do for you and your family.

Chapter 7
AuthenTIC

"I have drunken deep of joy, and I will taste no other wine tonight." – Percy Bysshe Shelley

Great therapy is like having your windows washed by a professional cleaning service. What you were only able to see through spots and smudges suddenly becomes crystal clear. For some of you, this might feel miraculous. "Wow, I never knew my backyard had that swing set. My entire summer is about to open up with endless possibilities for my children!"

For some of you, the clarity might be overwhelming. "Oh, God, I love the dog, but who knew the lawn had that much turd? How will I ever clean it all up?"

Not to fear, friends. No matter how dirty the windows of your life feel, the right professional can get you accustomed to your surroundings a little bit at a time.

For me, Sam was the squeegee to my dusty and dirty soul. I didn't always love the view he unveiled for me, but I knew in time, my eyes would adjust to the brightness. Sam presented a vision for my new life so I could give vision to Nicky's.

(And of course, second only to Sam was a great thrift store. There's nothing a 50% off Salvation Army Sale and a bin full of Barry Manilow records can't cure. At least for a few minutes.)

With only forty minutes to spare before picking up the kids, I should go home. Tics alone are unnerving. Add in some dirty dishes and unmade beds and I've got myself a recipe for serious frustration. But after my session with Sam today, I'm far too cheerful to waste my mood on housework.

From two blocks away my eye lands on a four-foot sign hanging off a double decker resale store. Super Thrift is my siren, and I gladly heed its call. Within moments my car is parked and I find myself on the second level, contentedly sifting through sixty-nine cent Children's Place onesies and two dollar Teva water shoes.

"A Pottery Barn art center for only nine ninety-nine?" I drop to the floor to get a better look.

A heavyset woman with a chenille blanket in her basket passes by. She looks admiringly at the table. "That's a good price," she says with a thick Russian accent. "You don't want it, I take it."

I haven't really decided either way, but knowing someone else out there is interested, I find myself saying,"Oh, I'm definitely buying it. Sorry." I smile and she smiles back. On the outside I am nothing but gracious. On the inside, I'm thinking, "Back off, Vladlina."

Likely she's thinking the same thing. Human nature is funny that way. How often do we complain about something or someone in our lives, only to find ourselves clinging even more tightly to it when we feel threatened?

"Do you want my son's T.S.?" I consider shouting back at her. "It'll last even longer than the table and you could have it for free!" That is one thing I don't want to keep for myself.

Shame runs through me, and it isn't because all my family's clothing is bought secondhand. I have no problem choosing to wear top brand designs for ninety percent off. That is plain smart shopping. My problem is how I deal with things I do *not* choose for myself. Like my reaction to T.S..

I think about my conversation with Sam today, and

within moments, my low mood begins to rise. I might not be happy about the tics, but so far, Nicky is happy with himself. That's more than I can say for myself.

As I sift through a large basin of wallets and belts my mind drifts back to his last year of preschool. Nicky had only recently been diagnosed. My nerves were raw. I was scared. What would the future hold for my little guy? Would he have friends? Would he be unable to read books due to unrelenting head shakes?

I was terrified and unsure of myself. The only thing I knew, beyond a shadow of a doubt, was that I loved this kid. I wasn't going to let my worries about his present and my own personal past destroy his future. If I had to fake it until I made it, that's exactly what I was going to do.

If the journey of a million miles begins with one step, then the first step had to be leveling with my kid. He had to know what he was dealing with.

With his sister already asleep in the next room, Nicky and I lay together on my king-size bed. It was about eight pm and we were just finishing up our prayers.

Aside from the occasional jaw thrust, Nicky's tics were very mild that evening. In fact, his tics had been nearly nonexistent for a month. "Maybe the doctors were wrong," I thought to myself, running my fingers through Nicky's hair. "Maybe he only had transitory tics and now they are gone."

As much as I wanted to believe this, I'd been through this cycle before. I knew that as sure as my love for Nicky, those tics would be back. I was not happy about it, but I knew I had to accept it.

"Let's finish up these prayers," I said cheerfully to my boy, frustration lingering just below my words.

"Thank you, God, for my Mommy," Nicky said, cuddling close.

"And thank you for Nicky," I added. I tickled the sweet chub under his neck. "How come you're so sweet?"

In between laughter he managed to answer, "'Cause God made me this way, silly Mommy!"

His answer revealed certainty, as if there was no other way for him to be.

"God also made you pretty darn smart," I continued. "In fact, He made you so smart, that sometimes your brain just goes around and around so fast, the only way to give it a break is to make a tic."

"A tic?" His face fell. "You mean black bloodsucking bugs are going to pop out of my head?"

Now it was my turn to laugh. "Not a t-i-c-k, Goofball. A t-i-c. It's a sound, or a body movement. It's also got another name. It's called Tourette's."

It might have been dark in the room, but I could see his face light up like a Christmas tree. "Oooooh!" he exploded. "I was wondering why I felt the need to do that. You mean, it's because I'm so smart?"

"Yes," I smiled. "And here's the real magic: God gave the tics to you, but He didn't give them to everyone else."

"You mean, not everyone's brain is made like mine?"

"That's right," I said. This was going better than I had anticipated. But that was Nicky – always finding the angle to make himself look good. "As you get older, kids might occasionally stare at the little sounds you make . . . you never know. But you don't want to make them feel bad by bragging about how brilliant you are. If they should ask, all you have to say is, 'It's my tic!' and leave it at that."

"That's very sneaky, Mama!" Nicky laughed, enjoying his newfound secret.

"It *is* sneaky, Nicky," I smiled back. "And it'll be just between us. Deal?"

He nodded his head, along with a confidential smile. "Deal."

Just like that I planted a seed of conspiracy. Beginning that night, all the way up until fourth grade, a strong flower of confidence began to grow. Some of this growth was due to the fact that as a mother, I was able to look beyond my own weeds and thorns and water this beautiful seedling.

But another part was due to the fact that my son – like all children – was a fertile ground for truth. We can choose to plant fear or we can choose to plant faith. We can choose to focus on the worms or we can choose to focus on the nutrients.

Like fertilizer in my son's soil, I added a good bit of manure to my pep talks. I knew at some point in life my kid would call me on it. But by the time he did, the self-esteem would have already taken root. I figured I could always do some pruning when the reality of his tic situation set in. But I couldn't add in glorious blooms of joy as easily.

There it was again – that word. Right then and there, amongst the piles of old purses and worn clothing, I made a contract with Joy.

"I, Andrea, commit to seeking joy in less than perfect circumstances. Like this table I am about to purchase, I vow to look beyond a few scratches and minor surface flaws. With a little TLC, I vow to repaint my life rather than throw it away just because something isn't perfect. I choose to overlook a few surface level flaws and commit to a good polish and shine. I vow to slow down and enjoy the process in the present, not worry about the outcome."

As I stand in line to pay for my table, I mentally sign my contract. My new life would begin this very moment. I am on top of the world. I could jump on that furniture and do a tap dance. It feels good. It feels better than good. It feels miraculous.

My cell phone rings, bringing me back to earth. "Hi, this is Jane from the school office. Your son is complaining of a sore throat. You need to pick him up."

"Oh . . . I'll . . . I'll be right there."

I click off the phone and set it in my purse. My eyes scan the line at the register. There are ten people ahead of me. There will be no time to pay for my treasure, let alone get it home and unload it before picking up my son.

I leave the table next to a rounder of tank tops and head out of the thrift store. As the door swings behind me, I look through the glass. Not surprisingly, the woman with the Russian accent is already picking up the table like a vulture descending on a wounded squirrel.

I try not to be annoyed. But I'm furious. Not only do I lose out on a bargain of a table, but my day is no longer my own. I now have to deal with getting my son early, taking him to the doctor, and finding a ride home for my daughter. Based on my son's pattern, I know a sore throat likely means strep throat, which means an exasperation of tics for at least two weeks once the antibiotics are finished – not to mention the tics will return stronger than before.

Joy turns to frustration and self-pity once again. As I fumble for the keys to my car, I mentally bring up my contract. This time I look at the fine print.

Your spirit is not going to transform overnight. You'll have a few moments of elation, but don't kid yourself. Most days – especially at the beginning – are still going to HURT.

As I turn the key in the ignition, a light pops onto my dashboard. It's the symbol of a gas tank, but what it really represents is my spirit. Its message is loud and clear. "Empty."

Takeways & Tips

- Make a pact with yourself to focus on joy – every day.
- Be prepared for roadblocks so you don't fall apart at every unexpected turn.
- Consider talking about T.S. with your child in a way that focuses on his gifts.
- Consider praying with your child. Giving control to a higher power takes pressure off you and your child.
- Enjoy the moments of stillness that punctuate T.S. Syndrome. It doesn't make you a bad mother to feel relieved that, for a time, there is silence.
- Find a hobby for yourself! If you don't thrift, find something else that you love. Tics are always changing, so find a passion that can serve as a constant funnel of pleasure.

Chapter 8
DiagnosTIC

"When you are a mother, you are never really alone in your thoughts. A mother always has to think twice, once for herself and once for her child." – Sophia Loren

If you're anything like I was, it can be hard for you to advocate for your child when you are face-to-face with a medical professional. Throw in a lab coat and a clipboard and you might as well grab that white flag out of your oversized mama-purse and scream, "Mayday, Mayday! I bow down to you, Doctor Ego. And while I'm prostrate on your cheap linoleum, take a close look at the fine print embroidered on the flag. It reads, 'You are smarter, more powerful and more educated than I am. My gut instincts about my kid's condition cannot compete with that diploma on your wall. Plus you are man which automatically gives you a fifty percent advantage. I surrender!' "

Listen to me, Mamas. You do have a voice. Your instincts about your child are not off. If you think something is wrong, it likely is. That said, try – as best you can – to keep your emotions in check or no one will take you seriously. It's not unlike someone feeding you a fancy seafood dinner. It can be lobster thermadore, but if they present it on a trash can lid, you won't want to touch it. Take a breath before you enter that doctor's office. (Then go kick some butt.)

Nicky does end up having strep.

Like many times before, we go to the doctor with no symptoms other than a sore throat.

Like many times before, I have to argue with the doctor about why I need a rapid strep test, despite no bumps or fever.

Like many times before, I have to bite my tongue when the nurse enters the room for the throat swab. She likely views me as an overprotective mother. She wouldn't be wrong.

Yet, like many times before, the throat test comes back positive. Everyone, except for Nicky and me, is completely shocked.

"We rarely see this," she tells me, clicking her tongue and going to get the doctor.

I think about PANDAS as a possible reason for his tics. He sure gets a lot of strep, and his tics certainly increase tenfold prior to antibiotics. Also, shortly after he receives antibiotics, his tics almost go away. Could Nicky have PANDAS?

To quote the National Institution of Mental Health's website, "PANDAS is an abbreviation for Pediatric Autoimmune Neuropsychiatric Disorders Associated with Streptococcal Infections. The term is used to describe a subset of children who have Obsessive Compulsive Disorder (OCD) and/or tic disorders such as Tourette Syndrome, and in whom symptoms worsen following strep infections such as "Strep throat" and Scarlet Fever."

Nicky doesn't have OCD, but it still gives me pause. Based on the amount of women I have seen pouring their hearts out on website boards like ACN.com, I'm not the only one who is confused and wants answers. PANDAS is relatively newly recognized disorder and remains very controversial among pediatric physicians and neurologists. No one knows exactly what exactly causes it.

I look up to the nurse, hoping to God she might provide a clue to this puzzle. "What do you know about PANDAS?" I ask.

"Never heard of it," she responds predictably. "Let me get the doctor to sign off on your Amoxicillin."

The good physician enters. He starts talking the moment he steps through the door. Clearly the nurse had informed him in advance of my question. He likely had other important things to deal with, like a two-hour lunch or chatting with other mothers who didn't waste his time with questions that made him think outside the HMO box. "I've heard of PANDAS," the doctor says, never giving me eye contact and handing me a pharmacy form, "But I'm not a hundred percent sure I buy into it."

Translation: "You were right about the strep, Hippie Mama, but I have a degree in medicine while you've spent the past seven years wiping butt and Ebaying used clothing for $49/month, hence this crappy insurance plan, so let me just cut to the chase and knock this out with some good drugs."

I push it a bit further. "Why does PANDAS seem so far-fetched?" I ask.

This time, he looks up from his clipboard and gives me the paternal stare down. "Take this with a grain of salt, Ma'am. I'm just the on-call doctor tonight and I have no idea what you've been through with your son. But I do know that there are a lot of parents out there who will do anything to feel like they are getting their kids on the neuro-typical bandwagon."

"Oh, like that crazy Jenny McCarthy with all her talk about autism?" I throw out. I don't think Jenny McCarthy is nuttier than anyone else pushing her healthcare platform, but if I need to see where a western medicine doctor's priorities lie, McCarthy is a pretty great litmus test.

This time he looks up, and he smiles. "Yeah, like her. Let her cure her kid the way she thinks is fit. For us? We stick to more traditional ways." He hands me the prescription.

It's six pm. I'm tired. I'd love to be a Jenny McCarthy warrior and tell this doctor to stick it where the sun don't shine, but my patience and finances are limited. Besides, Rite Aid closes at seven and it's a school night. Time is, like my kid, ticking. I'm over it.

***

On the way to the pharmacy, I vow to get more familiar with what PANDAS is (and isn't) so I can offer more helpful advice to other mothers in the future. Below is what I wish I knew then, but you get to learn now. Winner winner chicken dinner! Unlike Nicky with his strep, this is your lucky day.

What does PANDAS look like in a child?

Children usually have dramatic, "overnight" onset of symptoms, including motor or vocal tics, obsessions, and/or compulsions. In addition to these symptoms, children may also become moody, irritable or show concerns about separating from parents or loved ones. This abrupt onset is generally preceded by a Strep throat infection.

Is there a test for PANDAS?

No. The diagnosis of PANDAS is a clinical diagnosis, which means there are no lab tests that can diagnose PANDAS. Instead, clinicians use five diagnostic criteria for the diagnosis of PANDAS (see below). At the present time the clinical features of the illness are the only means of determining whether or not a child might have PANDAS.

What are the diagnostic criteria for PANDAS?

Diagnostic criteria are:

• *Presence of obsessive-compulsive disorder and/or a tic disorder*

• *Pediatric onset of symptoms (age 3 years to puberty)*

• *Episodic course of symptom severity*

• *Association with group A Beta-hemolytic streptococcal infection (a positive throat culture for strep or history of Scarlet Fever)*

• Association with neurological abnormalities (motoric hyperactivity, or adventitious movements, such as choreiform movements).

If a child resembles all five bullet points above, what separates them from kids who just have Tourette's and OCD and not PANDAS?

*Many kids with OCD or tics have good days and bad days, or even good weeks and bad weeks. However, **patients with PANDAS have a very sudden onset or worsening of their symptoms,** followed by a slow, gradual improvement. If they get another strep infection, their symptoms suddenly worsen again. The increased symptom severity usually persists for at least several weeks, but may last for several months or longer. The tics or OCD then seem to gradually fade away, and the children often enjoy a few weeks or several months without problems. When they have another strep throat infection the tics or OCD return just as suddenly and dramatically as they did previously.*

What other symptoms are associated with PANDAS episodes that might not occur just with Tourette's?

1. *ADHD symptoms (hyperactivity, inattention, fidgety)*

2. *Separation anxiety (child is "clingy" and has difficulty separating from his/her caregivers; for example, the child may not want to be in a different room in the house from his/her parents)*

3. *Mood changes (irritability, sadness, emotional liability)*

4. *Sleep disturbance*

5. *Night- time bed wetting and/or day- time urinary frequency*

6.   *Fine/gross motor changes (e.g. changes in handwriting)*

7.   *Joint pains.*

My child has had strep throat before, and he has tics and/or OCD. Does that mean he has PANDAS?

No. Many children have OCD and/or tics, and almost all school aged children get strep throat at some point in their lives. In fact, the average grade-school student will have 2 – 3 strep throat infections each year. PANDAS is considered when there is a very close relationship between the abrupt onset or worsening or OCD and/or tics, and a preceding strep infection. If strep is found in conjunction with two or three episodes of OCD/tics, then it may be that the child has PANDAS.

For more information on PANDAS, I highly recommend you check out ACN Latitudes. Their forum is very active and can provide you with much more detail than I possibly can.

Takeways & Tips

- Make ACN Latitudes your friend. This site has more info on tics, Tourette's, ADHD and PANDAS than you'll be able to digest in one sitting.
  - Full disclosure: I do NOT work or write for them but I do admire them greatly. Unlike my tendency to whine, moan and complain about a disorder I can't cure, these people take a more pragmatic approach to treatment. (But I'm funnier, especially when I'm not having a panic attack outside Kaiser Permanete worrying if the popsicle I just gave my kid is going to cause him to quack like a duck at the park pond. The people at ACN would never be so dramatic.)

- Google The National Institute of Mental Health and put PANDAS in the search bar. They, like ACN Latitudes, are a rich source of information.

- Consider reading Bethany Allison Maloney's book, *Saving Sammy*, in which she writes about successfully treating her son for PANDAS.

- Get your child tested by a trusted doctor to see if he or she is a carrier for strep.

- Insist on a throat swab to test for strep if your child or son has a sore throat. Bumps don't always indicate strep, especially in a child who has Tourette's.

- Have your child's titers tested to determine the level of antibodies in your child's bloodstream and the level of infection that may or may not be present

- Rest and take care of yourself, mama. You will get through this! If you aren't healthy, you can't be healthy for your child!

Chapter 9
NeuroTIC

"Medicine is not only a science; it is also an art. It does not consist of compounding pills and plasters; it deals with the very processes of life, which must be understood before they may be guided."
~ Paracelus

Whenever my son was on antibiotics, be it for strep or another illness, the tics cleared up. We're talking vanished quicker than a bunch of punk rockers at a Taylor Swift concert. At the time, I didn't know the reasoning for the symptoms sudden disappearance act. I only knew that I was relieved.

In retrospect, I can now clearly see how co-dependent I was on the tics. I had been basing my peace of mind on a medical condition that I had no idea how to manage. If that's not a recipe for crazy, I don't know what is.

I wish someone had told me what I'm about to tell you: It's okay to want to clear up the tics because obviously there is an imbalance occurring with your child's body, but be sure you are not obsessed with the tics because you, personally, have an imbalance. I'm not just talking about a chemical brain imbalance, which may or may not be the case. I'm talking about your expectations being out of balance.

The fact is, sometimes, as moms, we want so badly for our children to be okay that we forget that we have to be okay first. We allow the fears from our past to affect our kid's present and really, well, that's not helpful. If you think you might be doing this, you would be far from alone. But recognize it. Knowing the intention behind wanting to manage your kid's condition can make all the difference in how you treat it.

Bottom line: When you recognize that you are possibly projecting your own insecurities onto your child, your emotions become much more stable. Of course, I had to see a shrink, a psychologist and more churches than an evangelist on a Hillsong tour to learn this point, but I eventually did. (Just not in this chapter. But better late than never, right?) It's not too late for you, either. Promise!

Sure as white on rice, the antibiotics clear up Nicky's strep, along with his tics. We (let's face it, "I,") enjoy a two-week run with no movements or sounds. But Tourette's is like a loyal golden retriever. It always finds its way back to you.

"You just better pray it doesn't start barking or licking," says an inner voice in my head.

If a friend talked to me this way, I'd kick her to curb in an instant. Unluckily for me, this particular companion resides inside my anxious mind, feeding on my fear. The more I try to get it to shut up, the more it rallies back, meaner than ever. It's kind of like having a school yard bully wandering uncensored through the jungle gym of my brain, jeering and chiding me when I'm feeling weakest. If only I could find a recess assistant to send it to the office. Unfortunately, the only person who can blow the whistle on this brat is me.

For kicks and giggles, I decide to name my mean girl voice Rhonda in honor of a kid that used to torture me in fourth grade. I vow to work harder on giving Rhonda her walking papers – something that can only happen when I start thinking more positively. But for now, she's my constant companion and I will have to make the best of it.

The same is true of Nicky's latest tic. Turns out an uncomfortable looking shudder landed on his face just as the first of the holiday cards landed in our mailbox.

"It's beginning to look a lot like Tic Mas . . ." I sigh to myself as I attempt to enjoy the merriment of holiday decorating with my daughter.

Evie and I hang Christmas lights while my son plays Mario on the computer next door. "Five more minutes!" I shout to him.

"Don't the lights look like candy?" Evie squeals in delight, pointing to the green and red blinking bulbs.

"Yummy!" I answer. "But look how much prettier they are this way." I quickly find the light control box and switch them to a motionless setting. After all, I worry that the blinking L.E.D.s will set off Nicky's eye rolls.

I look over at my sweet eight-year-old girl. She is so calm. So focused. Like the lights and, so unlike my son, she is so *still.*

I wonder if she senses that even when I am with her – attempting valiantly to marvel at her grace and elegance — I am always thinking about Nicky? I wonder if she will one day develop tics. I wonder if it is possible for once, just *once*, to enjoy a moment without thinking about Tourette's.

I stare at the star on top of the tree. With a lovely glow emanating through cloudy glass, it reminds me of the journey taken so long ago. Despite uncertainty and fear, three wise men followed a shining star to push darkness out of the world. It gives me hope that one day my own darkness will be lifted when Tourette's is cured. But when will that be? And what the heck causes this disorder?

I had recently read that too much time spent playing video games could overload a child's brain with dopamine, causing him to twitch in rebellion.

"So much for staying in the moment," Rhonda retorts.

"All I can do is my best," I answer silently, all the while

faking a laugh for my daughter, who is giggling over a jiving Grinch figurine.

Rhonda continues in her own Grinchy way. "Why don't you just get a prescription for Haldol and be done with it?"

"I loathe the tics," I answer back, "But I'm not giving my kid meds."

***

Later that evening, when the kids are nestled, snug in their beds, I once again run through the drug options with Rex.

"So we're doing the right thing not giving Nic drugs, right?" I sip my wine, basking in the silence. "I mean, a prescription for Haldol is just a phone call away."

"Sweetie, we've been through this a million times. Unless it's impacting him socially or academically, he doesn't need it."

"It's impacting *me*!" I quip back.

Rex just chuckles. "True. Perhaps we should get *you* a prescription for Haldol."

Point taken. As much as I want a break from tics, Haldol is a bit extreme.

What is Haldol?

*Taken from the generic name Haloperidol, it's an antipsychotic medication used to control tics and vocal utterances that are part of **Tourette's Syndrome**. It works by interfering with the effects of neurotransmitters in the brain — the chemical messengers that nerves manufacture and release to communicate with one another. Haldol blocks receptors for the neurotransmitters (specifically the dopamine and serotonin type 2 receptors) on the nerves. As a result, the nerves are not "activated" by the neurotransmitters released by other nerves.*

The good news? It's been known to stop tics in their tracks.

The bad news? Haldol has some pretty serious side effects including, but not limited to:

- Irregular and fast heart beats
- Difficulty swallowing or breathing, tongue or mouth problems, including a tongue that protrudes from the mouth, unusual tongue movements
- Uncontrollable movements of the mouth, face or jaw
- Seizures
- Vision problems and severe eye pain
- Skin rashes
- Yellowing of the skin
- Erection that last for hours

"The side effects make tics look like a walk in the park, don't they?" Rex offered.

I nodded my head in agreement. We simply couldn't take the chance on meds. Puberty was around the corner. He'd have enough acne and hormones to contend with. We didn't need to be throwing yellowed skin and 24-hour woodies into the mix. Still, I needed to know we could do something, should the tics get worse.

"What if Nick starts emitting ear shattering howls, like that kid we saw featured on Twenty-Twenty last week?"

"It wasn't Twenty-Twenty," he informs me. "It was something you found on YouTube at 2am and forwarded to me during my business meeting last Monday. You could have at least told me to turn the sound down. Though those kids' screams were perfect background noise for the budget cuts I was presenting."

"I'm glad you're not concerned," I snap back, dejectedly thinking back to Nicky's latest tic – a shudder shake. "But you never know what could happen. What if the OCD portion of T.S. kicks in and he is compelled to shriek Yankee Doodle Dandy and do a high-kick march every time he sees a blonde-haired child?"

At that, Rex howls with laughter, catching his breath only long enough to say, "I wonder who he'd inherit the OCD from?"

I wish I had my husband's lighthearted attitude toward Nicky's condition, but fear sometimes rules me.

"Hey, at least I didn't send you the documentary on DBS," I tell him, shrugging my shoulders.

"What, pray tell, is that?" he asks, settling in for the big explanation. What I shared with him was a recap of this:

DBS – Deep Brain Stimulation

DBS is used only in the most extreme cases of Tourette's. It involves implanting electrodes within certain areas of the sufferer's brain. These electrodes produce electrical impulses that regulate abnormal impulses. Or, the electrical impulses can affect certain cells and chemicals within the brain. The amount of stimulation in deep brain stimulation is controlled by a pacemaker-like device placed under the skin in the upper chest. A wire that travels under your skin connects this device to the electrodes in the brain.

"Isn't that a bit extreme?" he clucks, not rattled in the least by my story.

"Perhaps," I admit. "I mean, some people might view drilling into their kid's head as insanely terrifying, but I feel a bit relieved knowing it's an option. I mean, it's nice to know we can face stuff head on . . . no pun intended."

"Babe, you've got to let this go," Rex sighs.

"I can't," I admit.

I think about my options. Being in this predicament is kind of like finding oneself in the mid-section of "Tics Blow Lane" and "Suck It Up Avenue." This middle road is uncomfortable, because not only do I not know how I got here in the first place — *what caused the T.S.???* — but there are a thousand signs leading me out. Which one do I follow? How do I know it's the right way? And how do I convince my husband that this isn't just about making *me* feel better, but it's about getting a good treatment plan in place for Nicky's future?

"I want to see a naturopath," I finally inform my husband, when he is well into his second glass of wine. "I know you don't think it's necessary. And I know you don't want to spend the money. But I've heard great things about this guy through your sister's friend, who heard about it through her cousin's uncle who was at her baby shower last month, and she says her daughter – who had degenerative hearing since birth – experienced a fifty percent hearing improvement just based on simple diet changes and it's something I feel compelled to do."

When I ramble, Rex gets quiet. It's not the best pattern, but it's all ours. I wait with baited breath for a response.

"If I say yes, can we stop talking about tics for the night?" Rex sighs.

"Absolutely," I answer back.

"Book the appointment."

Takeways & Tips

- In considering drugs vs. alternative medicine, weigh all the side effects.
- Consider the following question before deciding what route to take: Are the tics affecting your child emotionally, physically or academically? If not, you have time to explore more natural options should you choose pharmaceuticals.

- Stop Googling. Seriously, stop it. It's only going to drive you nuts. You need a plan, not a nervous breakdown.

- If you and your partner are on different pages about tics, unless your kid is going to die or is clearly upset by his tics, really try and understand your spouse's viewpoint. This is not because yours isn't important. It's because a peaceful home has a stronger impact on a child than a warring one.

- As tempting as it can be to look at the worse case scenario (Deep! Brain! Stimulation!) try and stay in the moment. No good decisions are ever made out of fear, anxiety or worry.

- Go easy on yourself, okay? Do I need to say that enough?

Chapter 10

HolisTIC

"Doctors?" said Ron, looking startled. "Those Muggle nutters that cut people up?" ~ J.K. Rowling, *Harry Potter and the Order of the Phoenix*

Finding a natural practitioner was one of the best things I could have done for my child during the particularly intense time this book covers. The advice I received from this wonderful healer not only stabilized my son, it helped to stabilize me.

Let's face it: Tourette's is a disorder that is constantly changing. Since I couldn't cure it, having a plan to manage it was at the very least encouraging. I simply wasn't comfortable dolling out supplements to my child just because some mom on a forum swore that Taurine was a miracle elixir. I found it better to spend a little money on an educated opinion than take my chance on an herb that might keep my kid from gulping but have him drop dead of a heart attack.

Bonus: If you happen to find a doctor as good looking as Nicky's practitioner, Dr. Carson, that doesn't hurt. But, based on what we all know about tics, looks can be deceiving. If you find a practitioner who looks like a smurf with warts, but he or she knows what they're doing, work with them. It can make such a difference on your journey to have a strong trail guide. Besides, it's impossible to be sad when someone is tra-la-laaaing about your son in an office shaped like a giant mushroom.

Four weeks later I find myself sitting on a round stool next to yet another exam table.

"What I'm going to do is place these little glass vials on

your chest and then see if your arm goes floppy."

"That's silly," Nicky smiles, flexing his muscle like a professional wrestler.

Dr. Carson, a kind and gentle alternative medicine doctor in his mid-thirties (who is very very cute but I already told you that) plays along.

"I know," he says, "But I'm a chiropractic kinesiologist, and we have superhero powers. That means I can take a teeny tiny jar of any food imaginable and, just by seeing how your body reacts to it, I'll know if you're allergic to it."

After a month of fighting with my husband about shelling out money for this visit — which it turns out isn't covered by our HMO — I'm suddenly relieved Rex isn't here. If the Buddha statue in the entryway, the herbal supplements at the front desk, or the soft harp music playing through hidden speakers didn't daunt him, Dr. Carson's unconventional exam room would cause Rex's head to spin off his shoulders. It's expensive enough dealing with tics. An exorcist would deplete our retirement.

"I sense healing and transformation," I could picture myself whispering to Rex. "We've arrived."

"I sense voodoo and unicorns," he would shout back, *"Ruuuuun!"*

For all intents and purposes, I couldn't blame Rex or anyone else for being a bit skeptical. To my right is an antique medicine chest housing vitamins and more jars of oil than a lighthouse. Scented candles sit atop bookshelves with titles like "Healing the Gut for Health" and "Right Brain/Left Brain Balance."

Rhonda simply cannot restrain herself. "How do you know this guy isn't just some snake oil salesman preying on desperate mothers?"

Rhonda has a good point, but if there's any chance

Doctor Carson can help, I'm willing to try. It's not like the traditional doctors have any answers. Worse case, I am wrong. I'm out a hundred bucks and I'll have a funny story to tell at cocktail parties.

Best case, I am right, I'll be out a hell of a lot more money for future visits, but I'll have peace of mind. You can't put a price tag on that.

"A lot of people who visit me for the first time aren't sure what to make of my practice," Dr. Carson says, pulling out a tool that looks halfway between a ray gun and a hand held ear piercer.

"What's to worry about? It's not like you are playing with jars of potions and are about to staple gun my kid's skull."

Doctor Carson, who is now placing the tip of this device at Nicky's neck, smiles. "This device helps realign the vertebrae in the neck. Come feel this."

He takes my hands and places them a bit below Nicky's ears. Do you feel how there's a knot here but not here?"

I gently massage Nicky's neck. "Yeah . . . I do."

"This tool will help realign Nicky's spinal column so his whole system is more in balance." He turns to Nicky. "I promise it won't hurt."

With that, he starts tapping on Nicky's neck. One time, two times, three times.

Nicky giggles, "It feels like a woodpecker." he tells Doctor Carson. "This is fun!"

"Getting your body healthy doesn't have to hurt," he says. "We're going to make you feel better than you have in a long time."

Hearing those last words sounds amazing, but it seems more farfetched than deep brain stimulation. Vials? Woodpeckers? It's all too hippie-dippie for me.

"That's because it *is* hippie-dippie." Rhonda interjects.

"Hey, look over there. Do you see that?"

"What?" I turn to look out the window.

"Your sanity. You've lost it. Go find it."

"I will," I answer back. "But I'm not leaving here without answers."

I turn to Doctor Carson, who is showing Nicky how to raise one arm to the left while looking over his shoulder to the right.

"So, I just have to ask . . . not that I don't trust you, but . . . ."

"What am I doing?" Doctor Carson is completely unshaken.

"Wow, in addition to chiropractic magic, you're a mind reader," I jab.

"I wouldn't say mind reader, but to answer your question, I'm helping rewire Nicky's brain right now. His eyes tend to dart to the left a lot, so by having him do measured exercises with his right arm, we're stimulating the left side of his brain to create neuropathways that bridge over to the right side. This means more balance where he isn't favoring his left side and he's less likely to shift his eyes. He'll be more centered."

I had read recently that the brain never stops growing. By creating new neuropathways we can get our brains more healthy. It still seems a bit mystical to me. I want to know more.

"I get that you're a chiropractor," I say, as Doctor Carson starts stretching out Nicky's back, but where does the kinesiology part come into practice? I mean, what is it?"

"In a nutshell, kinesiology works along the same premise as acupuncture, in that we view the body as a unit full of energy. That energy needs someplace to go. When something is off in the body, the energy gets stagnant. In order to figure out what is causing the block, we do muscle testing."

"The vials?"

"Yes. Unlike a regular visit to an allergist who does a skin test to determine if someone is allergic, we look for allergens in the body. Those allergens might not show up on a skin test, but it doesn't mean they aren't still in your body causing problems. By placing a small amount of the offending item in a glass vial, it sends just enough of a signal to your body to allow it to react. The premise is that if your body is not allergic, your muscle will stay flexed. If it is allergic, it will go limp."

"I thought if someone was allergic to something they got hives or vomited or got super bloated," I say. My mind darts briefly to a kid at my son's preschool who was so allergic to even the dust of peanuts that the teachers had to stand by with an epi pen just in case his throat closed up. It kind of put a buzz kill over snack time.

"It's a total misconception in our culture now that only severe reactions mean someone is allergic. Just because someone isn't upchucking their pizza doesn't mean their body can handle the dough and cheese. Like a drop of water on a hill, at first it's not a big deal. But after enough time, you're going to have a landslide of toxic buildup."

"So, that's where the muscle testing comes in that you were doing when you started today?"

"Exactly. Muscle testing is super helpful for pinpointing food intolerances that aren't as extreme as what you suggested, but they can wreak havoc over someone's body over a longer period of time. Removing the offending foods improves digestion."

Thinking about digestive health, my "gut" reaction is that this all makes sense.

"That was the worst joke yet," Rhonda chimes in.

"Careful, sweetheart," I tell her. "If this kinesiology stuff works, I'll be having Doctor Carson clear you out in no time. I see a vial with your name written all over it."

Rhonda settles right down.

I take a deep breath and watch this man – a stranger only an hour ago – placing his hands over my boy's exposed limbs. It's beautiful and intimate. It also doesn't escape me that my precious boy, normally a ball of wiggles, is calm and relaxed. If what Doctor Carson says about energy is true, I'm quite certain that Nicky feels nurturing and love oozing out of this practitioner.

A sense of comfort washes over me. Call it the scent of the candles going to my head, but for the first time since this journey began, I feel a sense of peace. I trust this Doctor Carson. He isn't handing me a pill to eradicate the tics. He's looking at the way the entire body works. It makes sense to me that once Nicky's body is aligned, it will be more balanced. A more balanced body means fewer tics. I'm on board.

"So what do we do next?" I ask.

"The next thing to do is start eliminating any toxins from Nicky's diet. Based on my exam, he's most allergic to eggs, dairy and wheat."

"That's his entire diet!" I was aghast. What would I feed this kid? Cardboard and monkey grass?

"I'm not saying it's going to be easy, but it's doable. You can switch from cow's milk to rice milk. There are a ton of gluten free products on the market. He can't have eggs, but flaxseed makes a nice alternative to yeast.

"I can't boil water, let alone bake bread," I gasp.

"Start small. You can get a lot of premade gluten free bread at the market. Eventually you can try your hand at using a bread machine."

"What about desserts?" I ask.

"Oooh desserts! I love ice-cream!" Nicky interjects. "And Twizzlers."

"Ixnay on the Twizzlers, bud. Those things are full of wheat. Plus the red dye in them can really mess up your brain."

Oh, I wish that stupid nutritionist were here for that last part.

"What about smoothies?" Doc Carson says.

"Yummy," Nicky licks his lips. "I especially like the strawberry ones my sister makes in Mommy's mini blender."

I briefly go inward to rewrite my Adventure Script. After all, the Tic Wrangler definitely has a face now – none other than Doctor Carson's sweet Irish mug. The silver bullets in his holster are replaced with two of my mini blenders – none other than Magic Bullets. This script is getting very exciting.

"That's awesome about liking smoothies," Dr. Carson continues, "Because your sis can start making more for special treats. Not only do they taste delicious, but they will make you strong and healthy."

"This all sounds good to me," I say with all sincerity, "But my husband is less . . . open-minded." Rhonda translation: "Rex is going to poop a brick, and we're not talking the hardened loaf of gluten free sourdough that will come from your invisible bread machine."

"I understand your husband's concerns. I hear it all the time. Heck, I myself was raised on the idea that milk makes a person strong and healthy."

"Are you saying the *Got Milk* campaign is a media-based lie?" I tease him.

"I will give those big corporations the benefit of the doubt that they just don't know the science behind the milk," the doctor smiles.

"Which is . . . " I prod him for more.

"Which is that cows have four stomachs to digest milk.

Humans have one. Some of us are able to process the milk, but others, like Nicky, cannot. The casein – the protein in the cow's milk – has no place to go, so it's forced back in the blood. Same thing with the gluten in the bread. The gluten, which is the 'glue' that makes the bread doughy, can wreak havoc on sensitive stomachs."

"And his body senses this foreign substance as an invading enemy . . . "

"And what does that enemy do to respond?" Doc Carson looks at me pointedly.

"It tics." My mind is now whirling.

"Bingo!" Doctor Carson says.

Nicky starts in with a low "Mmmm" sound.

"Clearing the dairy out of his system should show a significant improvement in his vocals," Doctor Carson says. "There will be less mucus buildup in his body, so his nose will clear out and he will be able to breathe better."

I love the concept of less dairy meaning less noises, but I'm not sure a tic-free kid with osteoporosis from calcium deficiency is a good tradeoff.

"What about making sure he gets the nutrients he needs?" I pipe in.

"Good point," Doctor Carson says, writing a list out for me. "He's a growing child, so whatever is taken out must be put back in. This should be through a ton of leafy greens and supplements. In addition to these food changes, I'd like to see Nicky on a good multivitamin that has a two-to-one calcium to magnesium ratio."

I sigh. I don't mean to be so loud about it, but it's all a bit overwhelming.

"That's the third time in ten minutes I've heard you sigh," Dr. Carson interjects, "Seems like a tic to me. Add in a physical quirk and you just might get diagnosed with

Tourette's."

"Here's a body jerk for you." I throw up the middle finger at him.

Dr. Carson laughs. He might have pulled a funny, but no one's funnier than I am. And with the big diet changes I'm about to embark on, I'm going to need a sense of humor.

Takeaways & Tips

• If you're interested in going the natural route before trying meds, finding a naturopath you trust can make all the difference in treating your child.

• If you can't afford a naturopath, consider this book – Sheila Roger's *Natural Treatments for Tics and Tourette's: A Patient and Family Guide.* This guidebook explains how to treat tics and Tourette's syndrome using natural and alternative therapies. This extensive book includes:

    o   Nutritional therapy

    o   Behavioral and counseling therapies

    o   EEG biofeedback

    o   Homeopathy to bodywork

    o   Energy medicine

    o   Chinese medicine (and more)

• If you don't relate to the first doctor you meet, don't stop until you find the correct one.

• Consider seeing a doctor without your child so you can talk without worrying about hurting your child's feelings.

• Stay open-minded to new techniques. Just because you haven't heard of something doesn't mean it doesn't work.

• Get referrals from other people to be sure you're not being taken advantage of.

Bonus Takeaways and Tips (because you're extra lucky with this chapter!)

• Consider a pediatrician that specializes in environmental health.

- Tip: When interviewing doctor's offices, many will not specialize in "Tourette's" so be sure to dig deeper: Here are some questions you can ask:
  - Do they treat tic disorders?
  - Do they understand nutrition?
  - What is their stance on food allergies?
  - Will they look at the child as a whole rather than treating the symptoms only?
  - What are their thoughts on alternative treatments like acupuncture, cranio sacral massage, meditation, cognitive behavior therapy, supplements, etc?

Chapter 11
TIC Tac Dough
"Let food be thy medicine and medicine be thy food."
~ Hippocrates

If you think giving birth is difficult, it's nothing compared to creating a new food routine for your family. And sadly, unlike birth, there is no epidural available when the pain gets too great. You just have to breathe, take rests in between the shouting, and have faith that a beautiful new life will be the result of your efforts.

If you're anything like I was, grinning and bearing the agony isn't going to cut it. Wine might work for a time, but after a while, you might find yourself needing something else. As I already mentioned, that person for me was my therapist, Sam. What I didn't mention, however, was that Sam was a Christian therapist.

Before you put down this book in horror and scream, "Oh, no, she's one of those Christian doobage smokers who thinks Jesus is going to fix everything" just relax. I am as far from a Bible thumping crazy as my husband is from enjoying my gluten free bread (or being a Christian for that matter). But I will say that, at the time this book was written, I had a feeling that something other than myself was going to have to fix my issue. And, by "sinking feeling" I mean "drowning-in-despair-there-had-better-be-a-God-or-all-of-this-pain-is-meaningless" feeling.

When you get a feeling like that, it's not a bad idea to act on it. Maybe for you it means going back to temple or starting a meditation practice. For me, it meant finding out more about the God of my youth. In my case, this was Jesus. I needed to know that another human being, just like me, experienced joy and laughter, but more to the point, felt grief and anguish.

Being the "intellectual" that I was, just reading about Jesus wasn't enough. It's all well and good that the Bible talks about Jesus walking on the waves, but how would I weather the storms of my own life?

I needed more than head knowledge. I needed heart knowledge. I needed someone to role model for me. That was Sam. With humility, strength and a good deal of compassion, Sam was my "Jesus with Skin On." I hope you find your Sam, too.

Or at least a better recipe for gluten-free soy-cheese pizza. Mine coule be summed up in two words only:

Epic.

Fail.

The first thing I find myself doing, other than having a heated debate with Rex as to exactly why we spent a hundred dollars to be told we were going to have to change our entire way of eating based on a miniature tube muscle test, is to take inventory of my pantry and fridge. Anything that smacks of gluten or dairy has to go.

Goodbye food dyes! Goodbye artificial flavors! Sayonara to products with "natural flavorings" which, translated, really means "Unnatural food designed to make your kid twitch more than Michael Jackson on the set of a Pepsi Commercial."

It has been known to take me hours to embark upon house cleaning of any kind, but this chore lasts me thirty minutes total. Spurred on by a passion to clear my son of anything remotely resembling shakes, jerks and annoying warbles, I go to task like ants on candy.

Five garbage bags later, I have a nearly-empty fridge and pantry. It also occurs to me that I have absolutely nothing to feed my family for dinner that night. I had better go shopping.

First stop: Check out my bank statement.

Sadly, elves have not stopped by and deposited money into my checking account.

It is all too obvious I can't afford this. "Fifty seven dollars and sixty four cents."

For a brief moment, I consider chucking my ideals and buying fifty boxes of Mac N Cheese from the 99 Cent Store. That thought is quickly replaced with something more enticing, thanks to Rhonda: "Use your credit card and get some healthy food. You can always sell some stuff on Ebay for some more cash later or get a job to cover the extra expenses. What's a little extra money if it means helping your son?"

Rhonda is rarely helpful, but in this instance, that witch makes a lot of sense.

Within an hour I find myself at a market with food prices higher than my mortgage.

"Is bread really five ninety nine a loaf?" I ask a young man who wears his hair in cornrows and sports a Ziggy Marley tee shirt. "It's true," he answers, "And I won't lie. It tastes terrible. But if you toast it and add some cashew butter with rice milk to wash it down, it's not too bad."

What choice do I have? We have to eat. Clutching three loaves of bread that resemble mortar tile from my fourth grade California Mission project, some wonky bars of fake cheese, a few bags of organic fruit, some Magnesium and B12 supplements and "cookies" that resemble hockey pucks masquerading as Oreos, I exit the store. I am a hundred and thirty seven dollars poorer, but I am richer in hope. I finally have a plan.

Not that my kids appreciate it. Dinners those first few nights are a disaster.

"Why can't we just have real quesadillas?" they moan. Rex just picks at his plate which, to be honest, isn't all that different from what he does with my regular cooking.

"Because these corn tortillas with soy cheese are just as good and they're going to make you as strong as Popeye when he opens up a can of spinach!" I squawk back.

"We still don't like it!" they cry. I sense anger and uprising and mutiny. I bring out the big guns.

"Then don't eat," I respond.

There's silence for a moment as Evie and Nicky lock eyes with me. Like the 2012 Presidential Elections, it could swing either way. After all, the choices aren't awesome. Given just last month, however, when I stripped their rooms of everything but a mattress because they refused to clean up their toys, they don't want to chance not voting positively for my food.

They start nibbling.

Within days, the family adjusts to the food routine — not just at dinner, but at all times of the day.

Other kids at school might munch on Lunchables and sip Capri Suns. My kids dine on wheat-free bread, organic grapes and gluten-free rice crackers.

When Nicky's friend, Miss Z, has a mermaid birthday party complete with an expensive mall cookie cake, I send him with his very own five-dollar gluten-free dairy-free chocolate muffin.

"Aren't you afraid he's going to feel left out?" Miss Z's mom, Ellen, asks while all the other kids are knee deep in frosting and Nicky is licking the crumbs off a paper wrapper.

"I do worry about Nicky being considered a bit different due to his eating habits," I admit, "But I care a lot more about him being viewed as being based on his tics."

A pang of guilt runs through me. Ellen is in a wheelchair due to an auto accident that took place over twenty years ago. Lord knows she understands what it's like to stand out from

the crowd – or "sit out" as the case is. While every other parent
at school runs after their kids with forgotten lunch boxes and
permission slips, Ellen zooms into a handicapped parking
space. She either pushes herself like hell to catch up with Z, or
she simply yells at her impish pixie from the sidewalk, "MISS
ZEEEE! YOUR LUNCH!"

Sure, Ellen is really different than the other parents at
school. But it's not because of her wheelchair. It's because she
is larger than life. From the moment she meets someone, she
makes it outrageously clear that her lack of legs does not make
her less of a human being. As a professor at a major university,
she lectures three times a week on education and sexuality. She
surfs, skis, dives, and acts on television. She is a rabble-rouser
who spearheaded our charter school's art program. She was
the first handicapped model to do a full cover spread for
Playboy magazine.

In my head, I know that Ellen's disability is what gives
her the ability to live a larger life than most of us can dream of.
But in my heart, I also know that if some simple diet and
supplement changes could fuse her spine back together,
allowing her the chance to run alongside her daughter at the
next school-wide kids' run rather than sit on the sidelines and
cheer, she just might take the chance. And I'm close enough to
her to tell her that.

"You know, Ellen, that I don't think less of you because
of your disability . . . not for a second," I admit. "But I have to
give Nicky the opportunity to live outside his disability if I can."

"I don't disagree with you," she says, "But be sure you
find that line between doing this for him, and doing it for you.
Because honestly, Andrea, we don't see his tics like you do."

She hugs me.

"I know, Ellen. And I don't see your chair."

"Obviously," she snaps back, "Which is why every time I

come to your house you leave me in the bleepin' driveway. Get a ramp or remember to push your gimp friend up your walkway."

"Tics and you can be a real drag," I laugh.

"We're worth it," she responds before opening the door for the magician she hired for Z's party.

"I bet you wish you had a magic wand for Nicky's tics," Rhonda cackles while watching Nicky stare sadly at the peanut M & Ms.

Turns out I had one. After just two weeks on the gluten free/casein free diet, Nicky's tics vanished.

****

One month later, the tics are still at bay. I am beyond relieved.

That is, until I open up my Discover Card statement. After four weeks of shopping at high-priced food stores, as well as bi-monthly visits to Doctor Carson, my credit card has gone from a manageable sum of money that my husband can get on board with—a zero balance—to over eight hundred dollars. With me not working, it doesn't take a genius to figure out that within six months I'll have a massive amount of debt on my hands.

I am panicked. I have no idea how I'm going to pay for my son's health care routine, but I know that going back to where we were before is not an option.

I have a few choices. One of them includes getting a full-time job. The problem with this option is that I used to write for television. While the pay can be lucrative, it means being away from my family eighty hours per week while I write about other peoples' families. This seems about as unfathomable as giving my son unnaturally-colored Scooby snacks for his lunches.

Nope, it's back to plan B: Ebay. Why not buy a few items per week at a thrift store and then sell them for triple that amount on Ebay? I can do it on my own time in between taking care of the kids. Amazing!

It sounds good in theory, but in reality, I don't have adequate storage space for my bags of clothing. Within a few weeks my office starts to resemble a thrift store that's vomited used boutique ruffle dresses and Polo shirts. This aggravates my neatnick husband to no end.

"You have way more clothes in inventory than you have going out the door," Rex mentions over dinner one night.

I want to respond, "I have way more money on our credit card now than I have profit to pay it off." Instead, I just say, "You're right. I'm going to stop shopping and just concentrate on selling."

But of course that doesn't happen. Being the social creature that I am, I hate being stuck inside all day. What do I love to do most? Thrift store shopping! Before long I become the picture of a very cheap hoarder. Mountains of Goodwill clothes pile up quicker than my resentment over T.S..

Intellectually I know I'm crazy-making, but I can't seem to stop. I want what I want, despite reason. Perhaps there's a 12-step program for people like me. "Hi, I'm Andrea, and I'm a Delusional Thrift Store Shopping Combating Tics-aholic."

At least I have Sam.

***

"The tics are way better," I tell Sam one Wednesday afternoon."But Rex is still irritated with me."

"This is nothing a steaming plate of good old fashioned glutinous noodles can't fix," he offers.

"First of all, I'm the clever one," I snap back. "Second of all, it's not as easy as food. It's so much more. You don't have kids. You're married to a woman who works full-time. You have a nice sized income thanks to suckers like me who can't figure out how to manage their emotions or their kids, so you have no right to talk."

"Actually I do," Sam says, "This invoice right here proves it."

He shows me a bill, yet another item I'll have to figure out how to pay off. Maybe that vintage three-story Barbie townhouse I have sequestered under our bed will sell this weekend.

I once again consider quitting therapy. Why pay Sam a co-pay of fifty dollars every other week just to have me verbalize how far I've sunk down the rabbit hole? That money could be better spent on food for Nicky or for more visits to Doctor Carson. I can talk a big game about wanting to live a more balanced life, but in reality, what I really want is for Nicky to never tic again. That's the only thing that's going to ever give me peace.

"I totally know I owe you money, Sam," I say, "But let's face it – I don't have a lot of it now. So until I pay off what I already owe you, I am going to take a break from seeing you."

"Oh, this should be good," he says, settling back for my big announcement. "Let's hear it."

I clear my throat and get on with it. "There's not a darn thing you can do to stop Nicky's tics. As awesome as Nicky is doing now, they'll likely start up again. And when they do, I'll be angrier than before, not just with the shakes, but with Rex who doesn't understand why I'm so pissed off. That will make me Ebay even more furiously to gain an extra thirty two dollars and forty seven cents a week to go after more alternative treatments that may or may not work."

"Sounds like talking this out has really given you an epiphany," Sam says.

"I'm pretty good," I add, patting myself on the back for dramatic effect.

"So, with you and your husband handling Nicky's disorder differently, and none of your friends facing the same parenting challenges as you, who do you plan on bouncing these ideas off of on a bi-monthly basis?"

"That would be you, dork." I throw a balled up piece of paper at him. "Like my husband, do you think I'd ever really leave you?"

"Not for a second," Sam smiles. "And do you think I'm going to hammer you for fifty extra dollars right now when, in reality, I know you'll work all this out and get it to me when you're ready?"

"Not for a second," I smile back. I feel better already. Which feels amazing. But frankly, feeling this elated after only a five-minute conversation irks me to no end. I want to feel as comfortable in my own head as I do when I am with my therapist.

I want to be as comfortable with Nicky as I am with my non-ticking child.

I want to be comfortable with Nicky's teacher, who is still waiting for his letter about Nicky's diagnosis.

"I wrote that letter to Nicky's teacher this morning," I tell him. "It's in that ball of paper in your hands."

He begins to open the mangled letter.

"I debated whether or not I was disclosing too much information about Nicky."

"How so?" he asks, starting to scan it.

"Well, I wanted to be upfront about his symptoms, but I worried that in being so forthright I would somehow put him on the radar. Then I realized that, well, he *is on the radar.*"

"Like it or lump it, there's no point living in denial," Sam says. "And Lord knows you are not shy about your opinion." He clears his throat and reads. This is what it said.

Hi Mr. Parker –

I'm excited to set up a time to talk to you.

In a nutshell, Nicky has Tourette Syndrome, a neurological disorder that causes a person to make uncontrollable vocal and physical movements. While he has always been considered a minor case (no problems in Kinder through Third) it is slowly becoming more of a moderate case, which is typical of those pre-Junior High years.

We recently put him on a gluten-free/dairy-free diet, which we hope will help him concentrate. We're already seeing great results with his tics.

NOTE #1: For the record, I am not that hippie-dippie parent who will blame food for his behavior. He needs consequences and goals just like any other kid.

NOTE #2: That said, we also need positive rewards and incentives. I'd like to talk about a classroom strategy that will help you help him.

Thanks for listening. I am VERY VERY OPEN to your insight, frustration and positives on my son. (Did I say very open?) I adore him, obviously, and I really want him to shine.

Andrea

Sam looks up. "This is a great letter. Personable, yet informative. You explained it so well."

I nod. It's one of those half nods where I'm attempting to agree with him and bask in the compliment, but in reality, I'm feeling defeated.

Sam reads my facial expression as clearly as the letter in his hand. "Andrea, *really*. It's extremely well done. You're a good mama. You are really moving this right along. So . . . how about we end this in prayer?"

I always cringe when Sam suggests this. I know I need all the spiritual support I can get, but praying to an invisible God about very visible problems like tics and anxiety makes me uncomfortable. I *want* to believe that someone holy and perfect is looking out for my very imperfect and unholy fumblings through life. And yet, it seems so unfathomable. Why would God care about someone like me?

And yet, the alternative is so much worse. I'm not exactly a "believer," but I believe Sam believes, and for now, that's good enough. It has to be.

"Let's do this," I say.

As Sam starts in, my eyes dart around the room. I never

know exactly where to look when he prays, so I look down. My once neon-pink Kangaroo sneakers are now looking Pepto-dismal puke. The hole in the toe is as depressing as the thoughts about my bank account.

I look a little higher up and my eyes settle on my wedding ring. This time I don't look away. Despite Rex and my misunderstandings, that ring is shiny. Like the God I sometimes wonder about, there's something about the sparkling diamond that gives me hope.

"Dear God," Sam begins, "I ask you to be there for Andrea. I ask that the Holy Spirit surround Nicky's teacher as he reads the letter Andrea wrote today. I ask that this letter bring clarity to her family as they form a game plan for her precious son. I ask that her beautiful daughter, Evie, remains a constant source of companionship to her brother. I pray that Andrea's words, like the very words you left for us in the New Testament, be a source of good news . . . literally *Good News* . . . for her husband. I pray that she learns to trust you. That if someone like you can die on a cross and rise again, that her own communication with Rex can rise from the broken place it's in now. I pray that she learn to accept the things she can't change about her husband, but work just as hard on accepting herself. Help her to set boundaries. Help her to be strong. Help her to feel powerful."

"Help her to kick some butt," I interrupt.

"Like she said," he continues. "We ask this in your name, Amen."

"Amen," I say.

There's a moment of silence while a serenity – which even Rhonda can't deny – settles over me. It lasts for only thirty seconds.

"Well, Doctor Smartie, since you're so into praying, you can say a prayer for my meeting with the teachers tomorrow," I say.

"I will," he promises.

But I think he must have lied because, well, it went about as amazing as Atlanta at the end of the civil war.

Up in smoke.

Takeways & Tips

- When eliminating foods from your family's diet, be patient as you try new recipes.
- Make a plan and stick to it, even if for just one month at a time. Be ready to change the plan up until you find one that works for your family.
- Consider taking out one offending food per month rather than doing it all at once. It's not only easier on your family and you, but you'll be better able to track if something is working.
- Try to find that line between eliminating the tics for YOU verses for your child. (Is he or she okay with them? If so, slow down and consider your victories. They are adjusted.)
- Consider finding a food coach, nutritionist or someone who has gone down this path before to give you encouragement.
- Don't expect tics to magically disappear the moment you implement a new diet. If they do disappear, it might mean the diet is working. Congrats! Or it just might be the normal waxing and waning of the tics. (This tic thing – it's a cheeky little syndrome, isn't it?)
- If you can't pinpoint triggers for tics, instead consider it a victory that you are implementing a healthy lifestyle for your family.

- Going into debt over a new food regime isn't an amazing option for your relationship. Be on the same page with your partner as much as possible.
- Keep talking out your emotions with someone you trust.
- Stop putting off facing the truth, whether it's writing a letter to a teacher or making that doctor's appointment for a diagnosis.
- Pray more. Don't have God in your life? Maybe it's time to send him an invite to your pity party. I can promise that He will show up. And trust me – he won't be empty handed. He'll be the perfect guest who will mingle well with everyone, compliment your gluten dairy free pumpkin pie, truly listen and even bring a huge banquet of food to help you feed others.
- Still hate the idea of God? I get it, but consider telling your brain to take a hike and open up your heart on this one. Even with just a tiny opening God can work. Your own crazy head got you into this predicament. Maybe a higher power can guide you out. (Oh, stop throwing tomatoes at me. Unless they are GMO free tomatoes. Those suckers are expensive and I could use some for my gluten free pasta sauce later.)

Chapter 12
UnanTICipated

"What you're supposed to do when you don't like a thing is change it. If you can't change it, change the way you think about it. Don't complain." ~ Maya Angelou, Wouldn't Take Nothing for My Journey Now

If you're anything like me, you don't like being told what to do. Every instinct screams, "I know better than anyone else, and if you could just do exactly what I wanted when I wanted it, in the exact order I'm requesting it, we wouldn't have a problem, now would we?"

Even if you are willing to take advice when it comes to yourself, it's particularly difficult when it comes to your child – even if you asked for the advice in the first place. The mama bear in you might find yourself roaring: "Tell me I'm more screwed than Bob the Builder in a construction zone, but don't you dare tell me my child is messed up."

Even if the above reaction perfectly describes you in all your defensive glory, I'm going to assume that since you're reading this book, you're open to suggestions. With that in mind, I'm going to give you some advice that might sting, but that you need to hear. After all, if you're greatest thinking got you into this emotional mess over tics, maybe it's time to rely on someone else's thinking to get out of it.

As you brace yourself for this important piece of news **that will literally change the way you parent your child through this syndrome**, *please keep in mind that I have been where you are: angry, exhausted, vulnerable and scared. The*

truth: If a more defensive, freaked out Tourette's mama ever existed, I don't where she was – until you, that is.

Hooray! Fearful, whiny, moany and clueless you is so much like the old fearful, whiny, moany and clueless me. We have so much in common . . . in fact, I dare say we're now bvffs – best virtual female friends. And bvffs can be honest with each other, right? So here goes:

__All Important Life Changing Parenting Advice__: Your child is not you, so stop taking everything so personally and get on with raising your kid.

It's true. Most well-meaning people, from friends, family and educators, are not giving you advice because they think you or your child is a screw-up. They are giving you advice because they care about you and your child. From their objective viewpoint, they see something is off that needs to be addressed.

As hard as it is, you'll need to separate your feelings from the issue at hand. If you're anything like me, this can be challenging when your emotions are more up and down than an over-caffeinated pole dancer. It's hard to hear truth when you're dizzy from spinning and sliding. (Not to mention sticky.) It might feel like an attack on your parenting or your child, but I promise it isn't. It's meant to help your child.

Notice how I said "your child." This is not about you. As hard as this may be to accept, your child is on loan. His or her Tourette's is not a personal affront to you. It's their life, so it's time to take your ego out of the way so you can best raise them.

(Not that I listened to any of this when I was going through this. Maybe I can spare you some of the pain I went through. And if not, well, go ahead and get nuts and make it all about you. It's normal, but it's kind of like watching the Kardashians: lots of unnecessary drama without the amazing eyelashes and fashion.)

***

As I mentioned before, as reliable as Sam is, he must have forgotten to say that prayer, because this meeting has only been in session for two minutes when the vice principal, Miss Kay, interrupts our easygoing chatter about Nicky's academic prowess and good natured personality with the following statement:

"Mr. Parker and I think it's time to initiate paperwork for an IEP."

Standing for an "Individualized Education Plan" an IEP is utilized for kids who need extra support in school, whether mentally, academically or physically. For my wonderful school, it means nothing more than to honor each student's particular needs. But for me, it signifies failure, and I'm horrified.

I look over at Nicky's teacher, who nods in approval. I look over at Rex, who has the same expression as he might have if a waitress offered him a glass of water.

I want to be calm and relaxed. I want to act like this is no big deal.

I want to say, "Of course we'll initialize paperwork. There's no harm in seeing if we can get some extra support for my son."

Instead, I find crocodile tears welling up in my eyes. Which really sucks, because they don't stay in my eyes. They start falling down my cheeks.

In between choking on my emotion, I manage to say, "But . . . Nicky . . . is doing so well. He's barely ticking at all now."

Miss Kay hands me a box of tissues. There's comfort knowing she has three boxes. I can't be the only parent who goes through this.

Rex fumbles in his seat.

Mr. Parker interjects, "It's not about the tics, Andrea. We barely notice them in class. It's other things that haven't improved."

"Like his focus?" Rex asks.

I am shocked that a cheerleader doesn't burst into the room at this point and do a jig for my tight-lipped husband. "Gimme an 'O!' For Obvious!"

"Focus is one piece of the puzzle," The teacher says.

I desperately try to rescue this train that's careening off the track.

"Look, like the letter I wrote said, oftentimes part of Tourette's is either OCD or ADHD. He definitely doesn't have OCD, so that leaves ADHD. He's never been formally diagnosed, but I thought the diet was really helping his symptoms."

After a quiet moment, Mr. Parker adds, "Honestly, I don't see a lot of ADHD symptoms in him."

"A child doesn't have to run around in circles to have it . . . just like a kid who doesn't throw up his food doesn't mean he isn't allergic to wheat," I say.

I've moved away from the subject and am now offering a one-line glimpse into kinesiology and food allergies.

I sound crazy.

It's time to save this conversation. "Nicky obviously has less ADHD and more of the ADD variety."

"It's not just his focus that we have an issue with," Mr. Parker says.

"We?" I think. So there's been talk about my son with the principal well before this meeting? Does this just mean my school cares, or is it one giant conspiracy plan to make me look bad? I'm mad enough that I choose the second option. The third option, which I don't take, is to punch out my husband, who has exhausted his one effort at communication and has now taken the Fifth.

If this were a cartoon, Miss Kay would be tossing a giant life preserver to Mr. Parker to keep him bobbing above the choppy water of this ridiculous conversation. Instead, Miss Kay just adds, "Last year's teacher, Mr. Parker, and I have talked about Nicky at length."

Oh, so *three* people are talking about my family. I'm going to start convulsing. Right here in the office. If you put me on Doctor Carson's table, it would be clear that I AM SERIOUSLY ALLERGIC TO THIS NONSENSE. **I HATE EVERYONE.**

"It's more than his ability to pay attention that concerns us," Mr. Parker continues. "It's other areas of his development also. He doesn't seem to be maturing at the same rate as other kids. He gets stuck on certain topics and isn't able to transition like other kids."

"My husband isn't exactly an expert at flexibility," I say, "And it doesn't keep him from making a crap load of cash."

Rex doesn't react. Miss Kay and Mr. Parker half-heartedly smile. Too bad his third grade teacher wasn't invited to hear the joke also. She'd have loved it.

I internally kick myself for revealing my husband's income. Now the school will probably expect massive fund-raising donations.

Damnit.

"I know this is hard thing for you to accept," Miss Kay interjects, "But getting qualified for an IEP doesn't mean there's anything wrong with Nicky. It just means he needs some extra help for his special needs."

"Special needs?" Rhonda whispers. "This just gets better and better."

Rhonda can't stop smirking.

I can't stop crying.

It's really turning out to be a stellar day.

"What exactly are you insinuating here?" I say, trying not to sound confrontational. With my arms crossed tightly across my chest and my eyes burrowing into them like light sabers, I'm not all that convincing. "Do you think there's more than just tics going on? Like . . . my son . . . has something else?"

No one says a word.

"Oh come on," I sigh exasperated. "Do you think he has something going on like . . . Oh, I don't know . . . say . . . Aspergers?"

I say it really slow. "Assssss...burgers." I sound like I have a potty mouth and have a hankering for McDonalds.

Neither the principal nor the teacher blinks. My husband, who shows no emotion at all, just looks down at his IPod.

"We can't say that Nicky does or does not have autism," Miss Kay says.

Well that's comforting. NOT. A traitor tear escapes from my eye.

Rex fumbles in his pocket. I assume he is looking for a tissue for me. Instead, he pulls out a set of car keys.

"Do you have some place to go?" I ask in disbelief.

Shockingly, he answers in the affirmative. "I actually do," he says. "I should have been at work fifteen minutes ago. Sorry for the quick exit, everyone."

With that, he thanks the teachers and shakes their hands, gives me a quick kiss, and heads out the door.

If my brain starts spinning anymore, I'll start ticking. And trust me, it will be the coprolalia cursing variety.

"I know this is a lot to absorb," Miss Kay says, watching me stare flabbergasted after Rex's exit.

"What part?" I say, completely over trying to pretend I have any understanding of the past fifteen minutes.

"Nicky is a wonderful child," Mr. Parker says.

I want to respond, "Thank you. And for the record, when will I be receiving my bumper sticker that reads 'My Autistic

Ticking Child is Student of the Week at Shiny Happy Rainbow Charter?"

Instead, I look at him and say, "I know. He is awesome. And I appreciate all you have done for him so far this year."

Nicky really is amazing.

Mr. Parker really is a great educator.

Miss Kay really does believe it's Nicky, not a label, who matters. She reminds me of this as I leave the office. "Call me anytime," she says.

I nod in true appreciation. Our vice principal is the rare exception. When she says "Call me about anything," she actually means it.

But instead, one hour later, when I'm knee deep in self-pity, confusion and blind red fury over a twist I never saw coming, I opt not to call Miss Kay.

I call my husband instead.

I never call Rex during the day, because he's often tied up in intense meetings. We have an understanding that if I do phone, it's over something super-important.

Which today's phone call is.

It's 2:15PM. I know he's in the middle of a Skype conference with some I.T. director in Germany. But this call can't wait.

"What' up, sweetie." It's not a question exactly a question so much as a direct statement. Translated in Rexian, it means, "This better be important." Lucky for him, it is.

"I just wanted you to know that in addition to feeling like I'm going to have a mental breakdown any day now over Nicky's tics and his potential IEP, I am well on track to having us about eight grand in debt this time next year due to shopping and cooking for our special needs/twitching/possibly autistic son behind your back."

A long silence ensues, followed by the click of my

husband's cell phone ending the call.

Really, that went better than expected.

Takeways & Tips

- When going to school meetings, be open to new information and opinions from your educators.
- Go to school meetings with questions written down. It will help when emotions creep in – and they *will* creep in.
- Don't attend school meetings ready for war. Give educators the benefit of the doubt that they really want what is best for your child.
- Sometimes our spouses won't act in a way we would like. Consider mercy and forgiveness.
- Be kind to yourself. You are grieving the original vision you had for your child's education.
- Circle back to your support group during times like this so you focus on what is working, not just what isn't working.
- If you don't have a support group, this is a great opportunity to get one!

Chapter 13
EraTIC

"I wish you'd help me look into a more interesting
problem – namely, my sanity."
~ Kurt Vonnegut, *Welcome to the Monkey House*

*Given how amazing I handled that last teacher's meeting,
as well as the exemplary way I modeled grace and elegance with
my husband, I decided that perhaps it was time I visited a doctor.
By "doctor" I mean a "mental health professional." And by
"mental health professional" I mean a "psychiatrist."*

*I am being specific with the exact nature of the person I
visited for similar reasons that a heavy drinker might find
themselves at AA meetings. It doesn't help to say, "I'm Barbara, a
person who loves the taste of Cabernet and likes to hit squirrels
and cats on the way home from wine tasting. Or was that my
neighbor, Sheryl? I can't be sure. Either way, how nice to
socialize with you all – the apple fritters are outstanding!"*

*No, Barbara's best bet to finding relief from her addiction
was total honesty. "I'm Barbara and I'm an alcoholic."*

*Like Barbara, I found it imperative to stop pussyfooting
around my emotions. Only by being brutally honest with my
feelings could I begin to feel better. And only when I began to feel
better could I best raise my son. Translation: I would rather save
my butt than save my face.*

*Some of you might not feel as comfortable sharing with
the world about your journey toward the nut-job's office. If
you're more private by nature, that's totally fine. You don't need
to share your decision with anyone, but I implore you: Don't NOT
see a shrink for fear of what others will think. Unless these all-*

important "others" are going to raise your child, it's none of their business. Chances are that these "others" are hurting as much as you are, but are choosing not to do anything about it.

Whether your naysayers take a look in that mirror or turn out the lights, your light is not a reflection of their darkness. Shine on with your big bad self. Your life is about you. And you, my friend, are worth every bit of support. If you can't do it for you, at this time, do it for your child. A healthy, stable mom is more important than fixing tics. It really is.

(And then, when you're feeling more balanced, consider sharing your experience with another hurting mother. This doesn't make you a basket-case. This makes you a human being. Congratulations on being an amazing one!)

A few days later I find myself seated on a white leather sofa in an upscale office building. The exterior of the building isn't fancy, but the inside has been replenished with fresh paint, crisp carpeting and thick molding. If the doctor I'm seeing – a highly rated psychiatrist – can make my insides feel as cohesive as this building, I think I'd forgo the vanity of my outside appearance, too.

Why can't I be like this structure – iron and metal where nothing penetrates? Where are my steel enforcers so I don't fall down despite the shakes and tremors that seem to roll in harder and fiercer with each passing day – both my internal and Nicky's external ones?

I shake my head and sigh audibly. To hell with exteriors! Isn't it my obsessive penchant for external quirks that has landed my ruminating brain in this office in the first place?

In a vain effort to distract myself, I look over at the stack of magazines fanned out in semi-circular precision on the coffee table. *Ten Ways to Cure Gout,* one publication promises. It really *does* look easy, and so pretty, too. Just look at all those tinctures and herbs encased in a lovely toile box.

Sadly, life isn't a magazine that has all the answers tucked inside high-glossed pages. My son didn't come home from the hospital in a retro laundry basket as seen on page 24. My spouse has yet to bring me flowers on a Tuesday and wear a matching apron while we cook a vegan pasta buffet for eighteen of our closest friends such as presented on page 86.

"Not to mention, the muffin top you're sporting can't be smoothed out simply with a vertical pattern and spandex filler," Rhonda pipes in.

"Anything else helpful you have to say?" I ask Rhonda.

"Sure," she jumps in. "Despite being forty years old and ten pounds over your goal weight, you're actually quite attractive. You're kind and smart. You're not a bad mother. You're funny and charming. You're damn near brilliant when you want to be."

I smile wide. "Wow, Rhonda, really?"

"No, totally kidding," she laughs. "You're screwed."

The blood drains from my face. What if Rhonda is right? What if I really am jacked up?

Giving myself the benefit of the doubt that I didn't cause Nicky's genetic disorder . . . and going with the comforting thought that it takes two to create communication issues in marriage . . . I can't help but feel shame that somehow I'm not competent enough to handle it. I feel guilty that instead of making headway toward a solution for Nicky's IEP issue, I am freaking out over my own.

What is my problem? Other people don't get so overwhelmed in their grief that they can't get through the day. Why can't I just chill out? What happened to the simple pleasures in life anymore, like a good cup of coffee or a day out with a friend? Why is it always me – alone – with only my rambling brain for company? And frankly, despite what they say about making yourself your best friend, I'd ditch me if I could. I'm just too toxic to hang out with.

"You've got *me!*" Rhonda says with pride.

"That I do," I cringe. "But your company is not the way I want to start my day."

Take this morning, for example. While waiting for my daily Starbucks coffee, my eye landed on a woman a few tables down. Her hand rested on one of those three hundred dollar Bugaboo strollers. The child inside was blonde and coiffed, a mini version of her mother. In between checking her I-phone and shoveling organic applesauce into her toddler's mouth, the lady would giggle at a handsome gentleman sitting at the table with her. .

It's said that when you start comparing yourself to other people, it's best to – *enter high-pitched Bible Leader voice* - adopt an attitude of gratitude. It's also said that if you're trying to pay off some debt, the first thing to kick is an expensive caffeine habit.

Both of those things clearly weren't happening this morning. Instead, I started chugging my latte like the java addict I was and continued to focus with laser-light precision on the happy threesome. Their conversation flowed freely. It was punctuated with laughter and smiles. Their eyes showed love and connection. Their posture showed affection, comfort, ease and fondness. It was healthy and admirable.

"It's disgusting," Rhonda clarified. For once, I agreed with her.

The trio's conversation went something like this:

Woman: Brooklyn did the funniest thing in *Mommy and Me* today!

Man: Was it that thing when she crawls on all fours near the safety gate and pretends to be a cow? (Looking at Brooklyn) What does a cow say? What does a cow say?

Brooklyn: Meeooooooowwwwwwwwwwwwww!

Hysterical laughter from the doting parents.

Man: You are a silly-willy cutie-patootie, aren't you, my Brookie Wookie?

Big drips of milk slobber down Brooklyn's face and fall onto big chunks of muffin on the table.

Brooklyn: I CUTE!

Raucous laughter erupts from the gloating parents as the man takes out an iPhone - identical to the one his wife has - no doubt to update Brooklyn's adoring fans on his Facebook account. "Brooklyn is a cute little bean at Starbucks!" the update will likely read with instant gratification precision.

Translation: We have a better life than you suckers sitting at home in your fat pants reading about our Pinterest perfect life.

Woman: She drew this picture. (Takes out a crudely drawn shape of an animal with black and white dots on its back.)

Man: *Moooove* over, Mama! There's the cow! You are such a good artist, Brooklyn! (To woman:) She really does have a gift, sweetie.

Woman: We must sign her up for---

Woman/Man: Art Lessons!

They giggle at the symmetry of their brilliant thoughts.

Woman/Man: Jinx!

Woman: Stop!

Man: (Grabbing her hands) Never!

Woman: Tell Mama what the cow is saying?

Brooklyn: Cow say 'Love you, Mama!'

Man: (Feigning hurt:) What about me? I love you, too, sweetie!

Woman: And I love you, Henry!

"Well I hate you!" I wanted to scream. "I hate that you

named your kid after a dirty city. Why not name her Watts? Or Detroit?" I can't stop my vitriolic train of hate. "Why would you spend eight dollars on chocolate milk and cereal bars from a coffee shop when you could have gotten an entire case for the same price at Costco? And what's the deal with your stroller? Do you think that by somehow spending almost half of what your barista spends on her rent that somehow you're insuring your child against a lifetime of confusing disorders or headache? And let's face it, once kid number two comes along, or maybe number three, and you can't take one more argument over the remote control or who gets the first BPA free cup of non-genetically modified soymilk, you're going to be sitting right where I am watching some other sucker who is way happier and who has even better triceps!"

At this point in my fantasy I put my cardboard Starbucks heat holders on my wrists and stomp out like Wonder Woman. Of course I can't find the keys to my invisible car, but that's completely beside the point. I would have had my day in the sun and kicked her perfectly yoga toned ass.

"You really have some anger issues," Rhonda offers.

"I know," I concede, "But truthfully, I'm not jealous as much as I don't understand how everyone else seems so together."

"Just because they don't talk about it doesn't mean they're not going through the very same emotional rollercoaster as you are," a kind voice reasons with me. It is so unlike Rhonda's. And that's because it isn't.

Sitting across from me now is my psychiatrist, Dr. Stine. I don't know what I was expecting, but it certainly isn't a woman the same age as me. It isn't someone with kind shining eyes who laughs at my jokes. And it isn't someone who would take an hour to get to know my medical, family and personal history before she started talking medication of any kind.

"Do you think there's something inherently wrong with the fact that you landed in my office?" she asks me. "Because I don't pay rent on this place for just a few people. A lot of folks these days are stressed out."

"I know," I defer, "But I didn't think I would be one of those people."

"What kind of people?" she presses.

"Thoooose people." Channeling my inner Jennifer Aniston, I flip my hair and fan my hand out to represent all the crazy nut jobs that are weak enough to warrant uppers or downers or whatever it is that the good doctor prescribes to normalize us.

"This is a tough world," she continues. "I'm seeing more people than ever before. And while it's true that some people need to grow up, and some people are genetically wired for depression and anxiety . . . all sorts of inherited genetic conditions for that matter . . . the fact remains that we are a pretty unconnected culture."

"Not me. I have over three hundred Facebook friends," I snap.

"Impressive!" She smiles back. "How much do you want to wager that at least fifty of them have been to a psychiatrist?"

I give her a "one never knows" shoulder shrug.

"But then again," she continues, "Since Facebook is known for its honest posts, and you're so connected with those friends on a deep personal level, you'd likely know for yourself the exact number of people who have sought treatment."

"That lady is pure snark," Rhonda interjects. "I like her."

So do I. But against Rhonda's point, Dr. Stine isn't snarky so much as intuitive and sharp.

But I'm not ready to trust her yet.

The truth is that despite coming here with questions, I'm terrified of the answers. I'm scared that she's smart enough to see through my personality and see the real Andrea underneath. The Andrea that is vulnerable. And tired. And disappointed.

And yet . . . if I can allow her to see the hurt Andrea, maybe she'll find the other Andrea lingering underneath:

The hopeful Andrea.

The writer Andrea.

The Andrea with dreams and visions about a future that doesn't just involve school and marriage counselors.

The Andrea who laughs and cries for happiness and can't wait to wrap her arms around Rex and make love after a few too many glasses of wine and engage perfectly lovely strangers at coffee shops because she loves the human spirit so much she'd much rather converse with them about their life stories than make up preposterous ones to make herself feel better.

My mind is at war. Like my near panic attacks of late, it's fight or flight battling it out for the premiere spot.

Enter booming broadcaster voice: **Who's going to take the gold? The positive or the negative emotions? The trust or the distrust? The faith or the fear? It's a tough call, 49.9 against 50.1.**

With only a fraction of a percentage going toward making a healthy judgment call, I decide then and there to ignore the turmoil of doubt in my brain and go with my heart.

The bell goes off. The brain's been pinned . . . the heart wins!

"That's an odd choice, considering she's a head doctor," Rhonda points out.

Rhonda might be right, but she's not as friendly as Dr. Stine. Unlike my mean internal girlfriend, Dr. Stine seems to be a genuine person who isn't judging me for having a hailstorm of emotions. There's so much that I'm not confident about these days, but one thing I suddenly have total confidence in is this doctor – this warm soul of a woman who seems to get that things don't always go exactly as we want them to go. But it doesn't make us any less of a human. In fact, it makes us more so.

"You seem really hard on yourself," Dr. Stine says. "What's your thought life like?"

"My thought life?" I ask.

"Yeah. How do you see yourself?" she asks.

"I . . . well . . . I see myself as someone who used to be pretty together. You know . . . someone who wrote for TV and made money and had a pretty decent social life. But lately I don't recognize myself."

"How so?" she presses.

And with just those two words, "How so," I am given permission to expose Rhonda for the nightmare she really is.

"I barely recognize myself anymore. It's like I have this other person living inside my head that tells me all the things I'm doing wrong."

I look down at my lap, afraid that if I look up I'll see her running for her secretary. Perhaps at any second she'll shoot me a look of disgust or launch into a long list of possible explanations for my impending psychotic breakdown.

When nothing of the sort happens, my eyes find hers again. She is completely unfazed. The only thing she is doing is nodding her head, in a kind of "I get it" conspiracy.

"I don't hear actual voices," I clarify, "It's more like a steady tape of negativity that I can't turn off."

"Good to know," she smiles. "Tell me more."

So I do. And not just a little bit. All of it.

If this scene were a play, I'd no longer be sitting in a modern doctor's office. White walls would be exchanged for black damask wallpaper. A fireplace would substitute for Dr.

Stine's space heater. My running pants would be swapped for an 1890's cotton frock and the doctor would have on a velvet lady's dress.

Playing a kind Mrs. Temple to my orphaned Jane Eyre, this would be the "come to" moment: the moment where my character comes to the realization that her life is going to change. She might not know how, and she might be more scared than an orphan in a red room battling unseen ghosts and demons, but she knows that transformation is lingering below the surface. And it's glorious.

"I see a lot of women like you, just so you know," Doctor Stine goes on. "Women that feel overwhelmed with motherhood and marriage. It's not like before when we lived near our sisters and mothers and family members. We're not all shouldering life's burdens from the comfort zone of communal living. We're scattered. And scattered people make for scattered brains."

"And scattered brains make for tired brains," I continued.

"Correct." She went on. "And while there is a heck of a lot more science to the art of brain chemistry than I'm alluding to in this conversation, the simple truth is that lack of support leads to dysfunction."

I sigh and do a half-hearted nod. It says both, "I agree to the dysfunction level. I hate it."

"Disjointed feelings don't mean you're crazy, Andrea. It means you've been living in survival mode and you're exhausted."

"So, you don't think I need medication?" I shot back, relieved that maybe I dodged my biggest fear.

"Oh, I think you do," she said bluntly. "You're clinically depressed."

"That's comforting."

"Sorry to be the bearer of bad news. But the good news is that this is a totally manageable condition. We'll have you back to your old self in no time."

"I guess I was just hoping I could skate by without medication," I say.

"You could. You could also walk around your whole life with a bowling ball, but wouldn't it be easier just to put it down?"

"But what if my husband is the bowling ball? What if it's the Tourette's? Why should I medicate myself to accommodate Rex or the tics?"

"What's the alternative?" she asks. "Are you going to fix Tourette's?"

I shake my head in the negative.

"Is Rex going to change? Are you planning on leaving your marriage?"

More headshakes.

"Is what you've been doing so far working?"

Again, more headshakes. Maybe it's a tic. Maybe I can't help it.

"Maybe you're just a freak," Rhonda interjects.

"Maybe it's time you put a sock in it," I say to Rhonda.

"Like you can stop me," she threatens, calling what she thinks is my bluff.

"Some medication will help calm down that negative voice in your head, too," Dr. Stine says.

"*Noooooooooooooooooooooooo!*" Rhonda dramatically acts out a knife being thrust into her heart.

"I've named that voice Rhonda," I confess. "I say you start me on a super high dosage and we nuke that bitch."

Dr. Stine laughs, filling out a prescription. "No can do," she says. "We want you less sad, but we don't want you numb to life. Your creativity makes you who you are."

"I'm not feeling all that creative these days."

"You've named your depression 'Rhonda', she says. "You haven't lost yourself too much."

She hands me the paper. "I want you to start with fifty milligrams for a week, then add twenty five, then add another twenty five. It's going to take a few weeks to kick in, so be patient. I'd like to see you back in about a month. And of course, call my office any time if you experience negative side effects."

"Are there any positive side effects?" I ask her.

"Weight loss," she says.

I picture those ten pounds instantly melting away. And just like that, Rhonda starts to fade in frustration. The Zoloft is working already.

***

Just as the doctor said, it takes about two weeks before the cloud starts to lift, but lift it does. The tics still come and go. Rex and I still quibble over time and money. But my reaction to both is far more manageable.

"I feel more like my old self," I tell Sam, settling into his dark blue couch and adjusting one of the pillows.

"You look much more relaxed," he admits. "It's time for the next step."

"Next step?" I say, a bit surprised. "Can't I just sit back and float on my serotonin high for a little bit?"

Sam grins and shakes his head. "You're way too much of a type A-personality type for that." He looks me over with conviction. "A few more days and you'll be back to your neurotic, frustrated self."

"What are you suggesting? Pole dancing? Sewing? Maybe a cake decorating class?"

"Nah. Though my friend's wife takes a knitting class at a place that made me think of you and your love for words. It's called Stitch and Bitch."

"Which name are you referring to that resembles me?" I quip.

"The Stitch, of course. You're funny. And you're far too classy to be called a female dog."

"Good save," I say. "So spit it out. What's my next step?"

Sam gives me his most practiced stare down. "It's time to help others."

I practically spit out my coffee. "Are you kidding me? I'm barely treading water myself."

Sam holds his ground. "I know. Congratulations on the not drowning part, by the way." He offers me a high five.

I cross my arms in protest.

He is not deterred.

"It's time to share the lifeboat with someone else who is sinking. Not only will you help them, you'll help yourself, too."

"That seems so . . . altruistic," I sputter. "Where am I going to find other moms? There's not even a Tourette's support group in my area."

"Then start one. You're a (big air quotes) *blogger.* Start something online."

"But this is personal. I don't want every mom at my kid's school to know everything about my son's life."

As I say this, I almost roll my eyes. If anyone wears their heart on their sleeve, it's me. (Translation: I'm a blabbermouth. Keeping my business private is hardly my strong suit. But I won't let Sam feel the victory.)

"Start a private blog," he continues. "My colleague, a sex addiction specialist, has a men's group for guys trying to stay away from pornography. Each member has a password. They go online and chat completely confidentially. They support each other in their efforts to stay monogamous."

"So, what happens if one of the guys messes up and

lands face first in a hooker's lap? Does he get the *shaft*?" I snicker. "That must be a hard group to *handle*. A lot of *balls* in the air."

Sam's face turns red and he laughs. "It can be a hairy situation, yes," he chuckles. "But . . . if a guy slips, he does what we all do when we make mistakes."

"Drink?"

"He starts over," Sam confirms.

Sam makes a decent point, but I'm still a bit leery. It's not like I really know what I'm doing with any of this. And yet, something inside me agrees with Sam. A kind, gentle voice, so unlike Rhonda, nudges me.

"If you feel this way, there's a good chance other moms do, too."

"You could be right, Glinda," I silently think.

As in, "The Good Witch," Glinda is Rhonda's replacement, thanks to the Zoloft. Like her entrance into Oz in a translucent bubble, she represents all the positive thought bubbles that have recently made their entrance into my brain.

Occasionally Rhonda comes in with a machine gun to destroy those bubbles, but Glinda takes out her wand and they have at it. Rather than get alarmed, I find it a bit amusing not to take myself so seriously anymore. And really, what could be better than an internal cat fight between a schoolyard bully and a Munchkinland fairy?"

"Earth to Andrea," Sam says, snapping his fingers . "So, what do you think?"

"Well, I guess I could start a Google Group," I say, picturing myself borrowing Glinda's pink dress as I cast happiness spells across Tourette's Land. "I could put the word out through my public T.S. blog and see who is interested."

"That's the spirit!" he says. "Now all you have to do is name it. How about Tic Talk?"

"Meh," I yawn. "Boring. Done. All that's missing is a logo of a kitten hanging from a clock. Too smarmy."

"Point taken," Sam says, "You need something more your style. Something that says Tourette's, but says it with a little wit. Because, let's face it, with you as the leader, it's not going to be perfectly drawn nutrition charts and feel good clichés."

"How about Twitch and Bitch?" I offer, half joking, making a pun off his knitting comment.

"That's perfect!" He says, laughing out loud.

Then I laughed, too. No one would, in a million years, join that group.

Within one week I have fifteen members.

Takeways & Tips

- There is no shame in seeking a mental health professional. Some of you are pre-wired for anxiety/depression, while some of you have depression due to circumstances. Doesn't matter! What matters is that you are healthy for your family.

- Be sure to tell your doctor everything. If you aren't honest, she can't help you.

- If your psychiatrist does not have a good personality, find someone else. You need someone who can reach your soul as well as your mind.

- Not sure you can afford therapy? What can you give before up giving that up? If your therapist gives you peace and suggestions to change your mindset, that's more valuable than a new pair of jeans each month.

- Still can't afford it? You can't afford not to. Get online and Google free mental health. Either you need to figure out a way in your budget to get some or you can't afford it, which means you're eligible for some healthcare through the state.

- If this is too overwhelming for you, find someone who can help you find help. You can't advocate for your child if you're not willing to have someone advocate for you.

Chapter 14
AltruisTIC: Twitch and Bitch

""The purpose of life is not to be happy. It is to be useful,
to be honorable, to be compassionate, to have it make some
difference that you have lived and lived well."
~ Ralph Waldo Emerson

*When I was going through this particularly tough time,
the last thing I wanted to do was take care of other people. But
what I discovered, much to my delight, was that in helping
another person I was actually helping myself. It became
impossible for me to stew, ruminate and drown in self-pity when
I was offering a hug or a kind word to another human being.*

*To this day I live by that motto. Maybe you'll consider
waving the self-service flag, too. After all, if misery loves
company, why not sign up for a daily cocktail hour? Who doesn't
love a good party!*

Before I actually get my fifteen comrades in tics, I have
to invite them to join my group. This isn't exactly an easy task,
given I don't have a group and don't have any idea how to start
one. With Sam's Cheshire Cat grin at the forefront of my mind,
however, I sit down to create it.

As I fire up my computer, I take a cue from the tagline of
a school mom's email. It's a quote from Gandhi that advises,
"Be the change you want to see in the world."

I beam with internal pride that perhaps the holy man
himself would be proud of me for reaching out to other moms
in crisis. His self-sacrificing message is also the perfect excuse
to avoid filling out that mound of IEP paperwork on my desk.

(That Gandhi is so good.)

Within moments, my trusty friend Google appears on my home page. I type the words "Google Groups" into the search bar and am quickly delivered to a link. I click it and am asked to *Create a Title*.

Twitch and Bitch, I type in.

I'm shocked that the name is not taken and, after hesitating for a moment, I decide to go for it. If a mom can't have a sense of humor about this stuff, she's not going to be of any help to me or vice versa.

Describe Your Group, I am prompted.

A private forum for moms to talk about tics and Tourette Syndrome, I type.

"That's a great start!" Glinda offers. She's wearing a new frock. It's purple with huge butterfly sparkles. On her feet are tennis shoes with rainbow socks. She looks like the Punky Brewster offspring of Richard Simmons and Judy Garland. Blessing me with her wand of sunbeams, she squeals. "So good! You are sooooo good!"

"Thanks," I smile, happy for the inward vote of confidence.

"Keep going! *Oh my dear, keep going!* Invite those lovely mothers! Write your first post! I am telling you, your angel wings will arrive by midnight!"

"Cool beans," I respond. "Now if you'll let me get started—"

"I tell you, this is just the beginning of a great—"

I grab her wand and smack her on the head. "Cut the crap. I need to concentrate."

"Fair enough," Glinda chirps. "But watch the hair. I just got it blow dried."

She takes the wand back and readjusts her bouffant. And then, with a snap, she flies off on a pink sequined cloud. No amount of rain or blows to the head can darken her serotonin Technicolor. She has a manicure at nine.

I have no time for such primping. I need to change the world.

With little regard for my unkempt nails, I comb like lightening through my email folder for names of moms I've been in touch with over the past few years. Some of them I've met through my personal website, www.happilytickedoff.com. Some I've met through an article on tics that was published by a national parenting blog. Some I've met through an online forum.

While all of them are strangers, spread out over the world, I hold them as dear friends who I'm connected to by the common thread of Tourette Syndrome.

To invite members to your group, type in their emails and hit send, Google instructs.

I pause, a bit reluctant. "Do I really want to do this?"

While I greatly admire each of these women individually, none of them know each other. Mixing them all together could prove disastrous. Each has her own attitude about treatment. Each has her own very strong beliefs on school settings and discipline. At best, we will have a surprise first reunion on *The Oprah Winfrey Network,* making the audience bawl tears of joy over our melting pot approach to Tourette Syndrome.

At worst, we'll unravel into a band of virtual mudslingers. Instead of *The Mommy Wars,* we'll ignite *The Tic Wars*: Magnesium vs. Haldol for a bloody battle to the finish.

Going with the same heart over mind decision that I made at Dr. Stine's office, I decide to send those invites.

I'm spurred on by the image of a party I threw a few years back where my mommy friends mingled with my husband's work friends. Leather loafers stood side by side with open-toed Keen water shoes. A few heated arguments erupted over vegan patty protein versus the nutritional benefits of In-and-Out-double double cheeseburgers.

While an executive Republican papa and hipster mommy quibbled over pro-life vs. pro-choice, their kids bonded over ADHD-inducing Doritos in the jumpy tent. With orange mouths and shining eyes, they interrupted their parents, begging for play dates. To this day, the girls are best friends. Their parents still couldn't be more different, but their love for their children softened their attitudes toward each other. They have a mutual understanding to "agree to disagree and move on."

And isn't that the point of life? To not sweat the small stuff but allow each person to contribute his/her thoughts? To truly, deeply hear them? To not take things so personally? To be open-minded enough to keep what is valid and – here's the real trick – *kindly and gracefully* discard the rest?

"That's your philosophy, but it's certainly not how the rest of world feels," interjects a harsh voice. "I mean, really, Andrea, why even bother?"

"Rhonda?" I gulp, taken off guard. "How did you get in?"

"When the good witch is away, the bad witch will play."

"Not for long," I tell her. "You might have a valid point, but if I don't try to make a difference—to get people together for the common good of helping our kids—nothing will change."

"Are you trying to heal your kid, or just heal yourself?" Rhonda snaps.

"Ouch." I shudder, thinking back to Ellen's comment months earlier. "That stings, but it is also, dare I say, brilliant."

It's Rhonda's turn to be taken off guard. "Really?"

"Yes!" I exclaim. "I want to heal both of us. I want our children and us to find relief from this wacky condition. I want to learn to ride the unpredictable waves of tics and float along the surface of acceptance."

"Sounds very poetic," Rhonda says, taking out a small violin. "You should write a musical," she goads. "Even better, a country song. Screw the violin," she taunts. She sets it on fire, grabs her fiddle, and starts strumming to her man-made bonfire. "Dance, Andrea, Dance!"

"I will," I say, imagining myself doing a jig to this devil's jeering. I do an impromptu country song:

I'm tired of keeping Tourette's on a shelf
If we can't fix the tics, we can fix ourselves, ya'll!"

Rhonda throws her fiddle into the inferno. "That was so bad, I can't even stay to argue," she grunts. Instead of flying off on a pink sequined cloud, she dives head first into the fire. I'm just glad she's gone.

For once, though, her visit made a difference. I now have a motto for my group: *If you can't fix the tics, fix yourself.*

Like my friend's tagline by Gandhi, I include it at the end of my Twitch and Bitch invite, along with a motto I decide to adopt from a Twelve-Step Program. I change it to fit the needs of Tourette's mamas.

God, grant me the serenity to accept the tics I cannot change, the courage to change the tics I can, and the wisdom to know the difference.

***

While I wait for my responses to the invites, I figure this is as good a time as any to fill out Nicky's IEP paperwork. In less than an hour, I have everything completed.

Two things immediately strike me - a statement and a question.

1. It wasn't as painful as I thought it would be.
2. *Why* was it less painful?

Alongside this statement and question comes an

answer: hope.

For kicks and giggles I Google "Definition of Hope."

Hope: A feeling of expectation and desire for a certain thing to happen.

It's an "I get it" moment if I've ever had one. Nothing in my life has changed in the past hours, but my perspective has radically shifted. With the entrance of hope, I am no longer a tiny David oppressed by the giant of Tourette's. I am instead the slingshot of expectation that will rise above all circumstances and knock the giant to the ground.

With my aerial view I feel confident I can look down on my situation with more objectivity. I can anticipate changes and start to see patterns. I will view conflict as character building. And I will finally sense healing – if not for Nicky, for me and my group.

I'm a bit alarmed that it took me four years to get into my funk and one hour to get out of it, but I decide not to analyze it too much. I might feel higher than a sorority sister at a pot party, but that giant can come back at any time. I better make more progress before he pounds the crap out of me.

Looking at the first page of the IEP paperwork, I find a sticky with the phone number of a resource specialist. Vice principal Miss Kay recommended her to me at our last meeting. "She's wonderful and so knowledgeable,"she promised.

An hour ago I didn't even want to call my husband, let alone a complete stranger about my son's impending IEP, but suddenly I find myself picking up the phone.

"Kids Community Resources," a gentle voice answers. "This is Teri."

I'm pleasantly surprised. I didn't expect someone to answer, but I'm happy she did.

"Hi, Teri. My name is Andrea. I was given your name from Miss Kay at Our Neighborhood Charter School. She said you might be able to talk to me about the process of getting an IEP for my son."

"No problem," she says. "Tell me a bit about his background."

I give her the five-minute rundown. She gives me a twenty minute intake, following it up with, "I can definitely help you." Then she says, "How about we meet for coffee and go over some material?"

"Wow," I say. "Are you sure? I mean, without sounding like a total cheapskate, I don't have a lot of funds right now. And I don't want to take up too much time—"

"It's my job. And coffee isn't expensive if we don't meet at Starbucks," she reassures me. "So if you're game, I am, too."

I look at my watch. "How about Zeller Grocery? It's halfway between your office and where I live. Say, eleven before the lunch crowd?"

"That works," she says. "What day?"

"Tomorrow?" I offer.

"You're on!" And with that, we bid pleasant adieus.

That was easy. I'm not sure what to do with "easy." I'm excited, fearful, worried, and most of all, mentally exhausted. This inner-growth stuff is not for the faint of heart. I want to take a nap but my work is not done. In the time I spoke to Teri, five emails arrived in my inbox. The title of each subject line is the same: "Membership to Twitch and Bitch: Confirmed."

Now I've really done it.

***

Since I have my first few members, it's on to the next step. I log into Google Group.

Write your post, I am instructed.

Similar to my first pregnancy test, that announcement came quicker than I expected. But, like being knocked up, I figure I'm either writing about Tourette's or I'm not – there's no in between with this baby.

I title my initial thread: *Guidelines*. And then I begin.

I'm so happy you all accepted my invitation to walk this journey with me. Just a few guidelines before we get started:

- *Nothing is to be repeated or reprinted outside this forum.*
- *No topic is off limits.*
- *No amount of bitching about twitching is too much.*
- *If in doubt about support or judgment, choose support every time.*
- *It's a serious topic, but don't feel you have to be serious.*
- *Other topics are fine, too! (Unless we are talking about football, in which case I will drool all over the computer screen in a sports-induced coma unless football holds the cure to Tourette's, in which case I will pay more attention than a referee at the Super Bowl.)*

I realize this post isn't really asking for feedback. And so, not unlike my first marriage that had me in the church and out the divorce court quicker than I could say "I do," I knock out post number two.

"Good girl!" Glinda chimes in. "The first time never counts anyway." Her white teeth sparkle like Chicklets. She looks radiant in an aquamarine mini dress, fake lashes, glittered eye shadow and maroon matte lipstick. If I attempted that stunt I'd look like a drag queen. She looks like a cover girl for Mac makeup which, in a way, is the exact same thing.

"You are beautiful," I say. And I mean it. She looks at me, picks up a hand held mirror, winks at herself, then faces it toward me. "You're beautiful, too. Just look at you!"

I look in the mirror. For a moment, I see a tired woman with hair desperately in need of a cut and color. But then, I see words: "Go for it," shimmering from behind sparkling glass.

Instinctively I know it's my true spirit reflecting back at me: *Write from the heart. Don't second guess yourself. People are counting on you.*

"Okay, I will!" I shout, feeling joyful and confident, albeit a little silly for talking to a magic mirror.

"Get to it," Glinda says, grabbing the mirror from my hands and plopping herself on the desk inches from my keyboard. "I'll be right here while you type. Admiring myself . . . making a spa appointment and ordering sushi." And with that she picks up her Magic I-phone and settles in for the long haul.

So do I.

Without hesitation, I dive into that second post. I make the decision to be intentional with my few first words. Like any television show, the first bits of dialogue and story will set the tone for the rest of the action on this forum.

I'm not clear about a lot of things these days, but one thing I know is that I'm not looking for platitudes from other moms pretending everything is going to be perfect. I'm looking for honesty.

Did the girls from *Sex and the City* get together to talk about how perfect their lives were going? No. They rallied around each other, week after week, dishing on everything from infertility to marriage issues to sex problems. They were not afraid to cry, show anger, or express fear or disgust. The key to their connection was their authenticity. There was magic in their vulnerability. By being so open about their failings and character defects, they granted us permission to be less than perfect also.

Never to be underestimated, there was a good dose of humor thrown into their pity parties. And even better than that, there was promise or transformation. Those girls showed us that even in the pit of darkness, there is light, for at the end of a bad breakup or job loss was the promise of a new and exciting relationship or career in the future.

Yes, I want the same the same thing from my group, only instead of better sex, I want a better handle on tics.

This goal isn't exactly as sexy as the hunt for the hottest man in New York, but I don't care. Feeling more peaceful about life sounds pretty orgasmic to me.

Introductions

Hi. My name is Andrea. I have two kids, Nicky and Evie. Nicky is 9 and Evie is 8.

Nicky was diagnosed at four based on minor vocal and physical tics. Now they range from nonexistent to medium – mostly shoulder scrunching throat clears. He eats gluten and dairy free.

For a while this really seemed to work, but now, I'm not so sure. The vocals are back. I never know if it's the waxing and waning of tics or what I'm feeding him or doing or not doing. It's maddening.

I know in my head that it's not my fault when the tics come back, but in my heart, I feel like a failure. I'm hoping I'm not the only mom in the world who feels this way.

Before I became obsessed with the notion that I could fix Tourette's, I wrote for TV. I loved the vibe of the writers' room with its raucous jokes and late night punchiness. You never knew what to expect from any given week, and I thrived under the challenge. (Which is odd, because the unpredictability of tics really sets me off.)

Life used to be pretty glamorous. I had awesome hair, an awesome apartment, and an awesome paycheck. My bimonthly stipend shouted to the world, "I'm smart! I'm clever!" It was the measuring stick with which I judged my success.

Then my measuring stick became my two kids – which

was going great as long as they were perfectly behaved, healthy, and didn't have Cheerios wedged in their butt crack.

But then the tics set in. Which leads me to the present.

Now that I'm measuring my self-worth by Tourette's, things are kind of not as awesome. I know in my gut that I have set myself up with a ridiculous recipe for failure. I get that I need to base my self-worth on something other than my son's condition, but how?

I'm hoping this group can help me move forward. I am tired of being so angry all the time. I am ready to ease the tics a bit if I can, but I'm also ready to accept that my son has this disorder and that, as much as I hate to admit it, I might not be able to cure this beast.

I want the serenity to accept the tics I cannot change, change the tics I can, and have the wisdom to know the difference.

That's it! Thanks, girls! This is working already!
Andrea

Fifteen women eventually chime in with their introductions as the week moves on. I could write pages and pages about how their laughter, humor, empathy and honesty infused my very soul with joy and life. But for the sake of time, I'll leave you with some of the top quotes that helped me feel so much less alone.

- "I worry that my kid is going to be teased!"
- "My faith is getting me through. I swear, girls, go get some faith if you don't have it already!"
- "I live in a rural part of England, so finding a group out here is next to impossible. Andrea's blog has been a lifesaver. She's a warrior!"
- "I've never felt so hopeless."
- "I've never felt so helpless."

- "My husband thinks I'm NUTS to be so crazy about tics."
- "What's the deal with neurologists anyway? Do they understand it's okay to show some personality?"
- "My brother had Tourette's! My mom called it 'His little habits' like it was no big deal. It went away when he was 18."
- "When people tell me that at least my kid doesn't have cancer, I want to punch them in the throat."
- "I suffer from PTTD – Post Traumatic Tic Disorder!"

Along with supportive words and talks about spouses and marriage and divorce and food shopping and house cleaning we cover:

- Holistic approaches to T.S. including, but not limited to:
  - Cranial sacral massage
  - Acupuncture
  - Yoga
  - Meditation
  - Supplements
  - Diet
  - Siblings with T.S.
  - Home school vs. regular school
  - IEP's
  - Dental appliances that "cure" tics
  - Experimental programs that cost six thousand dollars but supposedly rewire the brain
  - Psychologists and psychiatrists (for us and them)

- o   Effects of screen time
- o   Biofeedback
- o   Cannibus oil (specifically CBD – the non habit forming essential oil of the pot plant that is doing wonders in managing symptoms.)
- o   BRT (Bio Resonance Technology)

. . . and more.

As time goes on, I put much of this on my Tourette's Website at www.HappilyTickedOff.com under the "Remedies for T.S." tab at the top.

(But let's get back to our regular scheduled programming, shall we?)

***

As planned, I have my first meeting with the resource specialist the next day.

"I brought a little something for you," she says, offering me a 3-ring binder.

"Some light reading material?" I quip.

"Just all the options you'll need to navigate the IEP process," she says.

She is kind and knowledgeable, empathetic but direct. She doesn't mince words and doesn't waste time. As I thumb through the binder, one that has been mass produced by the L.A. school system, I take solace in the fact that I'm not the only parent in need of support.

We discuss many things, from how having an IEP does not signify failure on my part, to how having an accurate diagnosis is crucial to getting a child the help he needs.

"I don't really think my son has Aspergers," I confide, holding back tears.

"He very well may not," she says, sensing my discomfort. "Between you and me and this huge book," she winks at me in conspiracy, "doctors are quick to over-diagnose children. The public school system pushes for it also."

"That just seems wrong," I blunder, halfway defiant. "Why should my kid go through life with a label just to make it easier on a teacher?"

"It's not as cut and dried as that," she says. "Look, I'll be honest with you. My own two girls have autism."

I sigh. I'm a total insensitive defensive moron. Teri continues to talk to me anyway.

"I was like you. I did everything I could with nutrition and vitamins and a strong solid exercise regime. But there was something off. I finally had them diagnosed by a respected psychologist, and while I went through a small mourning phase, I was relieved. I knew, with the right diagnosis, I was that much closer to getting them the support they needed."

"You mean at school?" I ask, hooked on her every word.

"Yes, at school. Their 'label' got them IEPs. IEPs meant their teachers couldn't just treat their issues as behavior problems. One has a 504, which allows her more time to take tests. Another has an aid to keep her on track with class projects. Right or wrong, there's only so much a public school can do to work with your child without the proper documentation."

As Teri talks, I deeply study her face. Her dark chocolate eyes show no hint of fear. Her brown arms are not folded against her body in protest. They rest casually in her lap. She says the word "autism" as if she were talking about the word "ballet." There is no shame, no sadness. Only love.

"You seem so together," I confess. "I want that, too. For me, and for Nicky."

"You'll get there," she reassures me. "I was once in your position, grasping for answers. But I promise you: Autism does not define a child, nor does Tourette's. But pretending that there is nothing wrong, just so you don't have to face it? That doesn't really work either."

I know she's right. And frankly, that scares the be-jeebies out of me. I want to run out of the grocery store café and throw that threeiring binder into the nearest trashcan.

Instead, when I got home, I laughed my arse off at two more threads from *Twitch and Bitch* members entitled, "I named my son's head nod 'Bob'" and "Why the Leap Frog tic needs to burn in hell."

And then I made an appointment with UCLA to see a world-famous psychiatrist for Nicky's tics and focus issues.

Part of me was feeling very brave and enlightened. The other part can best be described with the two words:

Holy.

Crap.

Takeways & Tips

- Finding a support group is the best thing you can do for yourself.
- Laugh! You're not laughing at the condition – you are laughing for the sake of enjoying life despite being scared.
- Don't be afraid to start a group on your own. Think of T.S. as a giant invitation to step out into the world and make a difference. Private Facebook groups can be an excellent option, too.
- Be real with safe people – it's the only way to heal.
- Don't be afraid to go beyond your own school to find help for your child. This doesn't mean you've failed, or that you have to take someone's advice. What it means is that you're open to solutions. Good for you!

- If there's a doctor out there you think can help you, call their office. Worst case, they will tell you no. Best case, they say yes, in which case, hang on! It's going to be quite a ride.
- Take this one day at a time. It can be overwhelming, so make the to-do list your friend. You won't get to all of it in one day, but knowing a task or appointment reminder is there can put you at ease.

Chapter 15
BallisTIC

"Angry people are not always wise."
~ Jane Austen, Pride and Prejudice

Just when you think you've got special needs dialed in, the poop hits the fan. They shouldn't call it special needs. They should call it special poop. Whether you turn that poop into fertilizer or a stink bomb is totally your call.

For a ~~type-A personality~~ control freak like me, the hardest part of handling the poop is the unknown. From landing my dream job to my dream spouse and my dream babies, I was used to getting what I wanted.

The truth is, of course, that life couldn't remain a continual looping scene from Mary Poppins. I could not just snap my fingers and make a doctor call me back. I couldn't just add sugar to my son's orange juice and watch his nose sniffs disappear like the robin at Mary's window. Not that I didn't try.

Over and over, guided by self-will run riot, I attempted to get what I wanted come hell or high water, only to fall flat on my face. Sometimes I'd bring my husband and kids along for the perilous downhill journey. Lucky for them, no one was seriously injured in the crash, but it wasn't something I wanted to repeat on a regular basis – especially when everyone was expecting a simple beach excursion and I ended up driving them off a cliff.

For the most part, I now live life like a careful driver, but there's still the occasional all-family fender bender. For those times, I employ the seatbelts of grace and the airbags of forgiveness. It's not that these skirmishes don't leave their marks on my bruised and battered ego, but instead of looking at them *as failures, I view them as reminders. The scratches don't often become scars. They serve to remind me, "Andrea, you're not perfect. Your family loves you. Time to love yourself."*

Do you love yourself? If not, you will. Until then, find someone else to love you and trust that they know what they're talking about – even if that someone is just me.

It's twelve pm on a Thursday in April. The Santa Susana winds have kicked into full gear, along with Nicky's vocal tics. The meeting with Nicky's psychiatrist – who I will call Dr. Silver (as in this is going to be my Silver Bullet answer to all things Tic and Tourette's) cannot come soon enough. Sadly, it's not for another few weeks.

Backed by what I'm hearing on my Twitch and Bitch board, I'm pretty certain that my conspiracy theory is true: Neurologists and shrinks everywhere have signed a joint contract with the words "Make 'Em Wait" written in bold letters across the top.

I'm none too happy about the current state of affairs. Every ten seconds Nicky makes a noise – low enough that you couldn't hear him in a crowded school auditorium, but loud enough that the kids at his class table take notice. It's relentless enough that his teacher, Mr. Parker, sends home an email. "No big deal," he writes, "But Nicky is making these sounds quite a bit. Maybe he's nervous about state testing?"

Other emails follow. "He's been super restless. Three times this week I had to send him out of the classroom for arguing and daydreaming to the extreme."

I'm not a big fan of Mr. Parker's discipline style. I've seen him get snarky more than a few times, not just with Nicky, but with other kids in class. *"Really?* You're getting up from your chair again? *Really?"* he'll cajole, each word rising with a decibel of irritation. "Didn't I just tell you to finish your reading log?"

And yet, with twenty-three other kids to wrangle, I don't blame him for losing patience. Lord knows I couldn't handle being a teacher.

"That's why you're not a teacher," Ellen tells me over a glass of vino one Friday night. "If Nicky or another kid in the class can't pay attention, maybe they need something more challenging to do. Maybe they're, I don't know, BORED."

Four other women chime in with opinions. None of these women have kids with Tourette's, but all of them are struggling with something. These women are intuitive, smart, and funny. Best of all, they are totally transparent with their own problems.

My motley crew met at Our Neighborhood School when our kids started kindergarten, and for the fifth year in a row, we've gathered around Ellen's and raised a toast to life, love and all things in between.

Self-entitled 'Whine and Wine' (clearly the in-person spinoff of Twitch and Bitch) this is – *hands down* - my favorite night of the week. No matter how rough my Saturday through Thursday is, Friday night always winks with light at the end of the dark tunnel. It whispers to my soul, *It's Gonna Be Fine. People Love You. You Are Not Alone.*

I'm not the only one who loves this tradition. My children are equally thrilled to know that every single Friday they get to let loose and play with their friends. And who wouldn't love Ellen's house? It's not huge, but it's a child's nirvana with its trampoline, swimming pool, pirate ship play area, and more dogs and cats than a rescue center.

Frankly, Ellen's home might as well be called a rescue center, because she singlehandedly saved four women from a life of loneliness. She took that chip off our shoulders and – like a good pet owner – inserted a different chip. But instead of putting it in our shoulder, she skillfully placed it in our hearts. In a world of separateness, where it's so easy to remain isolated and alone, Ellen's unconventional generosity and care ensured that even if we got lost on occasion, we would always have a safe home to rest and heal in.

Now let's get real: friendship is not always easy. Friends tell friends what they don't want to hear, and on more than a few occasions feathers have gotten ruffled. For me, that was perfect. I wasn't interested in people's personalities. I wasn't about making myself or anyone else look good. I wanted the real deal.

Standing on her soap box, from the vantage point of her wheelchair, Ellen was cut from the same cloth.

"You've got to stop worrying about your teacher's feelings and advocate for your kid," Ellen insisted, fueled by a less-than-pleasant experience with her daughter's teacher a few years prior.

I know she's right, but I'm not as bold as she is. I'm hesitant to complain to Mr. Parker. Unlike Ellen, who has a Master's in Education, I only have a Doctorate in thrift-store shopping. Ellen, despite being paralyzed from the neck down, has serious legs to stand on. I just have my gut instinct.

"And you're doing a great job," Ellen continues. "Nicky is an awesome kid. Maybe Mr. Parker isn't the right fit for him. The way I see it, most public schools are a holding tank at best. Ours is one of the better ones, but it's not perfect. You have to advocate for Nicky."

She's right, of course, but I'm just not ready to wave the mama bear flag yet. I have so much on my plate with the upcoming IEP meeting . . . with my communication issues with Rex.. . . . with the tics. I can't add, "Ask Miss Kay about switching teachers" to the mix. Not when, in my heart, I can't 100% blame Mr. Parker for being annoyed at Nicky.

His tics aside, Nicky has been exhibiting a restlessness at home that can only be described as hyperactivity plus. I'd like to deny that there's a problem, but I know otherwise. He can go from building Legos to reading a book to playing a card game all within a fifteen minute time period. If I ask him to clean up, he will either argue or say "sure" but then, halfway through sorting pieces, get distracted by something outside and take off, leaving the screen door open.

With all due respect to wiggly and jiggly nine-year-old boys, Nicky's intensity has recently surpassed a child's natural need for answers and instant gratification. It's been bordering on an intense nudging and opposition that cannot be squelched with reason, positive reinforcement or negative reinforcement.

I have considered the old school method of spanking him for every time he begged for more computer time, despite being given very clear guidelines in written and verbal form, but I'm quite certain that it would only result in a black and blue child who would – moments afterwards – ask me for a soft pillow for his sore butt to sit on and play more Mario.

After receiving the third email in a week from Mr. Parker, stating that he sent Nicky to the vice principal's office for droning on about video games instead of doing his times tables, I had my fill.

Delete.

It's not that I don't want to be kept in the loop, but the looping in my head is quite another thing altogether. It's the first time since the Zoloft that I've been overwhelmed with feelings of fear. I consider upping my dosage, but short of medicating myself into a flat-lined trance, it's just not realistic for me not to react. I'm just going to have to wait for his appointment with Dr. Silver.

"Oh, man, he didn't fall asleep until midnight last night," I yawn to Sam one afternoon. "This is the fifth night in a row.

Plus he can't get through a sentence without a click, clear, or strange sound that can only be described as a choking gulp. Occasionally, as if adding an exclamation for effect at the end of a sentence, he includes The Squeak."

"The Squeak?" Sam asks, clicking away on his laptop computer.

"Yeah," I say, shuddering at the thought. "It's the one sound I've always feared and now, like the elephant in the room, I can't ignore it any longer."

Sam's response reminds me of a quotation from a Passover ritual I hear every year at my best friend's parents' house. *What makes this night different from any other night?* "What makes this sound different from any other sound?" he asks.

"It's distinctive in that it can't be mistaken for a sound a normal kid makes," I groan. "Throat clears can be mistaken for having a dry mouth. Clicks can be construed as boredom ... kind of a tongue clucking replacement for humming." I "hum" out the theme music to the *Star Wars* theme song.

"I have no idea what tune you just clicked," Sam notes, "But I see your point. It sounds like something I do when I'm bored." He makes smacking sounds and taps his fingers on the monitor in illustration.

"Right!" I exclaim. "But Nicky's squeak? It's different. It resonates like bubbles boiled in the throat that slide down his windpipe and pop in his esophagus. It's just so..."

"Touretty?" Sam offers.

"Yeah," I nod. "*Tourettey*. I know I need to accept this. I mean, I get that he has this condition. But I was just kind of hoping that we could hide it from the public a little bit longer."

"Why? Because you're afraid he's going to be treated differently?"

"Yeah," I admit. "It would break my heart."

"What about your friend Ellen? What if she went through life trying to pretend she wasn't in a chair?"

"That's different," I say. "Ellen isn't my daughter. Not for one second do I judge her for it."

"How much do you want to make a bet that no one judges Nicky for his disability?" Sam says.

I know he's right. I recently met my friend from Twitch and Bitch, Tammy, whose son was thrusting his arm every thirty seconds. Tammy was so distraught over it that she left him with me for a last minute sleepover so she could have a mental break. Me? I took full advantage of Colin's tic by sticking him on my team for an impromptu game of back yard volleyball. His "little quirk" made for a hell of a serve and didn't bug me one iota.

Sam gazes at me intently. "Who hurt you when you were a little girl?" Sam says.

"Oh here we go," I say, already a mile ahead of him. "Is this the part where you try and tie in my reaction to Nicky's tics to the shame I felt when vicious school kids made fun of my height?" I snap.

"Didn't need to," he says. "You just did."

Sometimes I really hate that guy.

***

On the way home from Sam's, I think about what it was like to be teased as a kid . . . to be asked over and over "How tall are you?" or be the last one picked for the team. I can think of all the psychological wording on the planet to describe the feeling, but the best two words I can come up with are: It. Sucked.

Despite giving Sam a hard time, I know he's right. If I can get to the root of my own insecurities – if I can somehow forgive the *real* people who hurt me so badly in the past – I can stop fearing *imaginary* people that might hurt Nicky in the future.

And yet, getting to the root of shame is like trying to write about wind tunnels while sitting in the eye of a tornado. It's a near impossible task, for while one might have a birds-eye view of the storm, they become so dizzy from the twisting and turning it's hard to concentrate. Not to mention it can snap their spine in the process.

Someone from my Twitch and Bitch group put it brilliantly: "For me, a Tourette's diagnosis was kind of grieving my son's death. Only my son wasn't dead – just the dream I had for his life was dead. So while I'm still going through all the stages of grief, they're not necessarily in any order. Denial, anger, depression and acceptance are kind of all jumbled up together."

I couldn't agree more. And as much as I wished differently, anger was the stage I was in at the moment.

More than a few times on the car ride home, I try to make "The Squeak," but to no avail. It's impossible. It's a ticker's gift and not mine to recreate.

Hours pass after I pick up Nicky and Evie from school. With ten tics a minute, multiplied by four hours, that's an awful lot of noises to listen to.

While I'm about to lose my brain, Nicky is forever unbothered by it.

"Want to—*quack*—read a bit more—*gulp-gulp*—of Harry Potter with me—*throat clear*—*click-click*—*SQUEAK*?"

"No, sweetie, but I am sure your sister wants to hear more of the story, don't you, Evie?"

"I do!" says Evie, forever Nicky's cheerleader. Her abundant enthusiasm for Nicky's every move, twitches and vocals not withstanding, only make me feel guiltier for not wanting to be around him. I am a horrible human being.

Towards dinner, I can't contain my irritation a second

longer. Despite the heat outside, my oven is cranked up to 425 degrees . . . a lovely parallel for my red-hot agitation. Buckets of sweat drip down my face. I don't have the air conditioning on in attempt to save seventy-five cents on electricity. And yet, I'm not really saving money because this gluten free/dairy free pizza – half the size of a normal pie – cost me fifteen dollars. And for what? It's not going to cure the tics. If anything, it's going to make the kids cranky because it tastes worse than the box it came in and then I'm going to have to deal with noises on top of whining for real food and *I AM DONE!*

"Mama—*gulp*—I did my—*clic- click*—reading log so can I watch a little TV—"

"No!" I shout. The room, including all tics, gets silent. I slam the oven door. Nicky's eyes get wider than the circular tray the pizza cooks on.

"You cannot watch TV! Oh MY GOD! Just stop it!" I slam the oven door again and again in irritation. *Open, slam! Open, slam!* "Stop it! Stop it! Stop it! It's driving me crazy!!!!!!!"

"What is, Mama? What is driving you crazy?"

He's now crouching behind the kitchen stool. He looks like a dog about to be smacked for pooping on the carpet. I'm a jerk, no doubt, but I would never hit my child. At least not physically. Verbally is a whole other story. I can't stop the words from coming out.

"The noises! Can't you just stop with the tics! Just for a little bit?!"

Now I'm even more furious – not just at my son's tics, but at myself for losing my cool, as well as losing a perfectly good pizza. It's blacker than my mood. I open up the oven. The smell of burnt pizza dough fills the air.

Nicky twitches his nose at the smell but he says nothing. His brow remains frozen as he ponders my previous question. Just as quickly, his face opens up with an expression of unadulterated optimism.

"How about I take a Tic Tac?" he offers.

I'm stopped in my tracks.

"A what? For what?"

"I bet if you bought me a pack of those Tic Tacs like they have in the grocery store line I could control my tics a bit."

I look at my sweet boy, still clutching the remote control in his little hands.

"Come here," I say, dropping my oven mitt and collapsing on the kitchen stool.

He climbs into my lap and puts his head on my shoulder.

Gulp-gulp. Click-click. Little heart beating fast. Tears falling—mine, not his.

"Nicky," I begin, stroking his curls. "I know you can't help your little noises. And I shouldn't have screamed like that. But, is it possible to breathe through a few of them? You've been doing it almost a month. And, well, Mommy loves you so much but she just needs a break."

"I *can* stop–"he looks up, eyes wide with a longing to please.

"Great! That would be great!"

"But you know it's hard for me," he continues.

"I do," I admit. "But . . . well, I'm not a saint. After a while, I lose my patience. Maybe, just maybe . . . maybe we could consider getting you some medicine to calm it down just a bit? Because, you know . . . it's been kind of relentless."

"But Mommy! If we did that, the tics would go away!" Big crocodile tears fall down his face.

"So???" I answer in disbelief at what I'm hearing.

"So . . . it's how I was made!" he answers. Translation: Duh, idiot.

This is my chance to stop talking to just hold him in my arms and then send him on his way to watch mind-numbing television while I order a cheap gluten-filled pizza and let him tic to his heart's content. He loves himself! He is confident. I've created a child with a sense of worth. I win. Send me the award with a gold star of approval. I'm done.

Instead, I continue, "But I can't be the only one who gets frustrated at the sounds at times. Doesn't anyone ever get bugged in class?"

"Sometimes," he admits, his eyes lowered in what I perceive as sadness. But just as quickly his face takes on an expression of half defiance, half who-gives-a-crap bravado. "But that's their problem, not mine."

Then he jumps off the chair and looks up at me with the conviction of a preacher at a tent revival. "I have a great idea!" He says, putting my oven mitt in his hand and using it as a puppet. "Since I don't have a problem with my tics but *you* do, why don't YOU take the drugs?"

If there was ever a demonstration of a nine-year-old bitch-slapping his mother, this was it. And the humor could not be denied.

I smirk at first. I then start snickering. Before long, my snickers turn into unstoppable giggles, which transform into deep soulful belly laughs. Nicky looks at me like I've lost my marbles which, in reality, I have.

The fire alarm goes off. I am guffawing so hard I can't even bring myself to turn it off. I've gone through such a state of emotions – all in the course of five minutes – there's nothing I can do but sit still and let the smoke, like my laughter, rise into the air and take over the kitchen.

Nicky, however, has another idea. True to form, he takes full advantage of the chaos to sneak out of the room and flip on the TV. I'm in such a good mood, I don't even stop him. Instead, I smack down the snooze alarm – a layman's attempt at knocking out the batteries to silence the siren – and move into the living room to read.

When Rex comes home a few hours later, he finds two glassy eyed children on their third hour of Scooby Doo, a house that smells of charcoal, and a snoring wife who is passed out on the couch. He gently rubs my shoulder.

"Um, what's this?" he says.

"Just your madcap housewife living the life," I sigh, eyeballing the destruction.

"No, what's *this*?" He presents a white bottle he found on the counter.

Whoops. That was so supposed to stay hidden behind the Tumeric. "Tic Tamer," I admit – *solidly busted*. Already knowing his next question, I just spit it out, "I got it off the internet."

"Are you serious?" he sputters. "Do you know anything about this stuff?"

"Well, no," I admit.

"You could kill him!" he says, dumping the bottle in the trashcan.

I jump off the couch to retrieve it. "Don't do that! It cost twenty bucks!" I plead, attempting to avoid Yuban rinds and half n' half in my spastic attempt at retrieval. "I got it off a vitamin website. Loads of happy mom testimonials say it works wonders."

I cringe as I say that last part. Rex doesn't hide his irritation.

"Really?" he argues, arms crossed. "What's in it?"

"I don't know," I say truthfully. "It's why I want to see a nutritionist but you don't think we should spend the money--"

"Don't blame this one on me!" he interrupts, once again taking the bottle from my hands. This time he opens it and dumps the contents into a glass of water. Like my hopes for a tic cure, I watch the pills dissolve into tiny fragments of nothingness.

"Can you speak more quietly?" Nicky shouts back from the TV. "We can't hear Scooby!"

Oblivious to his son, Rex's voice continues to rise in irritation at me. "If my kid needed a heart transplant, I'd sell my kidney to get him the care he needs. But he isn't dying. He's not unhappy. *You* are the only one who's unhappy."

"I'm not unhappy!" I sob, tears running down my face.

My performance is so convincing, it's shocking I didn't win an Oscar. I suppose the Academy was saving it for the next day's encore.

***

The next morning, bright and early, I find myself seated side by side with Rex outside Miss Kay's office. I've got a pounding head from lack of sleep. Apparently drinking a bottle of wine by myself on the couch, while Rex slept upstairs, wasn't my best move either. And yet, it silenced my head, if only for a few hours.

With Rex focused on his i-Pod, I focus on the possible results of his IEP intake – a four-hour process, done over the course of a few days – where Nicky's critical thinking, social and academic skills were reviewed by a school psychologist. I don't know what to expect and, to put it mildly, I'm nervous.

"He's likely going to need a personal aid," jibes Rhonda.

"Who asked you to come along?" I quip, trying to shove her into the back of my mind.

"You'll be fine," chirps Glinda, pushing Rhonda aside with her parasol. "I even got a new dress for the occasion!"

She twirls and shimmies in an adorable polka dot A-line with coordinating patent leather pumps. She fans herself with an envelope purse, batting her long lashes towards my husband.

Rex is, as expected, dressed for success in a pair of crisp Dockers, white shirt (replete with his initials on the cuff) and shiny brown Oxfords. I'm in a Costco tank top, thrift store Gap jeans and flip-flops. I can almost hear my kids' favorite Sesame Street song piped through the speakers: *One of these things is not like the other...*

"Your husband is so dreamy," Glinda sighs.

"He really is," I think. As annoyed as I can get with our communication, there's no doubt that this messed-up Barbie landed herself one hot Ken. It doesn't make IEP meetings pleasant, but it helps.

Miss Kay's familiar face appears in her doorway.

"Come on in, Frazers!" she says brightly.

As we enter her office, I notice that Mr. Parker, is also seated there, along with a woman in a suit.

"Thanks for coming in, guys," Miss Kay says casually. "This is Irene Sanchez, the school psychologist who did Nicky's intake."

Rex and I both shake Irene's hand. On the outside I'm smiling. On the inside, my stomach is dropping faster and lower than the Tower of Terror – a lurching and plummeting elevator ride from Disney's California Adventure theme park. I just pray the meeting is over as fast as the ride and that I make it through the jolting parts without puking.

I look directly at Ms. Sanchez, bracing for the inevitable news that my son not only needs an IEP, but further testing.

"Your son was an absolute delight to work with," she says.

I don't say a word. I'm too busy keeping myself from falling off the chair. Glinda fans herself with delight. My husband stares straight ahead. Rhonda begins to fume.

"At first he was very nervous," she continues. "I'm glad Mr. Parker told me about the tics because they were in high gear the first fifteen minutes. But after that, they totally subsided. He is incredibly bright and creative, not to mention polite."

"This is so disappointing," Rhonda grimaces. "I'm outta here." With that she scales the walls and escapes through the ceiling tile.

As Ms. Sanchez goes on with her report—all good news—I briefly scan the office. I half expect Ashton Kutcher to jump out from behind Miss Kay's filing cabinet, screaming "You've been punked!"

"Nicky's verbal skills are through the roof. He's totally on top of his math. He's reading at an advanced grade level and his critical thinking skills are wonderful," she continues. She hands me a stack of formal looking documents.

"These are copies of his assessment," she says. "It's a lot, so feel free to contact me if you have any questions."

"Well, I have one now," I say, not even looking at the papers. "What about his focus?"

"What about it? He paid total attention and had little trouble staying on track."

I look at Rex, who is about as perplexed as I am. Mr. Parker, whose number one issue with him has just been taken off the table, shifts in his seat. I think back to his third grade teacher who had similar concerns for my little daydreamer. Secretly, I wish she were here as well for the big reveal. Where's my banner? "Congratulations! It's Not *Just* Your Child's Fault After All!"

Fueled by Ms. Sanchez's evaluation, I can't help but do an internal victory dance. I don't have to play it so safe anymore. I don't have to second guess what I had always thought about my kid: That perhaps, as great as his teachers have always been and are, he is a bit bored. Perhaps, despite some focus issues on his part, he also has a good deal of smarts to contend with. I just have to clarify one thing.

"So he doesn't need an IEP?" I ask Ms. Sanchez.

"Not at all," she says, quite confidently, adding, "Though if you want to do a private assessment, we can always reevaluate."

I mention that I am, indeed, taking Nicky to UCLA.

Mr. Parker stops shifting in his seat. He reaches under his chair and hands me a yellow envelope. "Here's the paperwork you had me fill out for the psychiatrist," he says.

I glance it over quickly. Many of the questions are related to Nicky's attention span and his behavior. One sentence stands out. "He doesn't always play well with others. He's a bit on the immature side."

I bristle but take a breath, making it a point not to take it as "negative" but instead as "constructive" feedback. I hope Mr. Parker will do the same once he hears what I have to say in front of the vice principal and the psychologist.

"I'm sure we'll figure out a way to calm him down some. In the meantime, since he's not eligible for an IEP, we're going to have to work on classroom management a bit more," I venture.

Mr. Parker sheepishly smiles. He starts to say something, but I continue with my statement.

"With all due respect, I've done everything you've asked me to do, from SSTs to IEP evaluations. But I don't always see that happening in the classroom on your end. I know my son isn't easy, but he's clearly very engaged when appropriately challenged."

I sense Mr. Parker starting to cringe. I feel bad. But this is my child. Channeling my inner Ellen, I continue to advocate. "I feel like you've spent an awful lot of time focusing on his flaws and not enough time focusing on his gifts."

"I love your son," Mr. Parker says, his face turning

redder than his hipster button-down shirt.

"So do I," I say. "Which is why I'm going to create a chart for you that helps you keep him on task."

"That's a great idea," Miss Kay says, trying to keep the conversation light. "What does he need to work the most on?" she says, directly at Mr. Parker. Her eye contact seems to say, "Attack! Attack! Avert the mother bombs!"

Mr. Parker takes the lifeline. "Well, he is obsessed with Mario. He talks about it all day." I sense the exhaustion in Mr. Parker's voice. "Once I had my friend come in and talk about law. I allowed the students to ask questions at the end. He put his hand up and asked if my friend liked to play Super Mario Galaxy. I told him, 'Nicky, this is not appropriate. We need to ask questions related to the legal market.' All my other students seemed to grasp this concept. I figured Nicky would get it also. So when he raised his hand again, I gave him a second chance. This time he asked about law relating to video gaming and if they affected the creation of Super Mario Galaxy."

I try not to laugh. The psychologist steps in.

"He brought up Mario with me, also. I found that if I simply redirected him, or incorporated it into the project, it wasn't really an issue."

The psychologist isn't making Mr. Parker look amazing, and I feel bad about it because Mr. Parker is a great teacher. But in this one area, he is having a hard time thinking outside the box.

So I created one for him.

The next day I hand him a chart consisting of one big box and five lines. One for every day of the week. There are three columns that read:

Before Recess/Before Lunch/After Recess. Across the top of the page read the following words: Mario Talk

NO MARIO TALK

	Mon	Tues	Wed	Thurs	Fri
Before Recess					
Before Lunch					
After Recess					

Nicky's goal is simple: He is not to utter the name of that damn plumber.

Not once.

Not even if a new student kid came in named Mario. He would have to refer to him as Paco.

Mr. Parker's goal is simple: For every period before recess, before lunch and before the end of school that Nicky did not mention Mario, he gets a star.

My goal is simple: Stars equals Nintendo time on Saturday and Sunday. Every star is worth five minutes. Every time he doesn't get a star, he loses ten minutes. If he doesn't complain about lost time, or goes out of his way to be helpful at home, he gets additional stars. If he asks me for additional stars based on what he thinks he earned, he loses everything. It's tough love at nine, Mario style.

This chart would prove to be a bit of a pain for Mr. Parker, and a bit of a pain for Nicky, but I'm the one who would have to drive my kid to UCLA in rush hour traffic with nonstop vocal tics. I had the greatest pain to deal with, and after waiting so long to see Dr. Silver, I didn't care.

In the end, all would be worth it: No pain, no gain. Mr.

Parker would gain some peace, Nicky would gain some gaming time, and I would put the final piece in the "How to Deal With Nicky's T.S." puzzle.

<u>Takeways & Tips</u>

- If you have a blowout and scream at your kid, they'll forgive you. I promise. (Just forgive yourself.)
- Consider what you can do for yourself that takes the pressure off so you don't have such meltdowns.
- Sometimes you have to go to bat for your kid with school administrators - no apologies needed.
- Come up with suggestions for your child's teacher so he can reach your child in ways he might not have been thinking about.
- If you come up with a behavior chart, stick to it!
- Discuss the behavior chart with your child in advance. Even better, have them create consequences so they know what they are in for.
- What is your child's currency – the thing they love most? Use that to barter for better behavior.
- Consider positive reinforcement.
- Stop overthinking if you're being too mean. It's easier to be strict and pull back than the other way around. And guess what, you're not doing your child any favors by being a softy when society expects more from them.
- You won't be the first person to fight with your spouse. Consider stepping away from a conflict before stepping away from a marriage. If you think tics suck, try dealing with it as a single mom.

Chapter 16
PyschiaTrIC

"Always laugh when you can. It is cheap medicine."
~ Lord Byron

It's one thing to go to a shrink for yourself. It's quite another to go for your child. By the time Nicky's big day arrived, I was more jumpy than a jackrabbit on steroids. But truthfully, I was also punchy. At some point, things just felt funny. How did my perfect dreams for my son end in a psychiatrist's office after spending two hours in bumper-to-bumper traffic? Humor saved me – not just then but in all parts of my parenting journey.

Maybe you're feeling a bit dark these days? If so, take care of yourself, take care of your child, and have some fun. If not for you and your spouse, stay lighthearted for your child. After all, you might find the cure for tics along the way, but you might not. Either way, you'll never regret teaching your child that life can be full of joy and hope despite less-than-pleasant circumstances.

Final tip: Fake it 'til you make it. Act as if. Your family and your own soul will thank you for it. And really, that chubby cross dresser in the mini skirt wearing the "I Love Nerds" tee shirt you met in the lobby of the shrink's office was hilarious. Don't miss those gems!

Our big psychiatrist appointment finally arrives. After a brief interchange with Rex, Nicky and myself, where Nicky informs Dr. Silver that "UCLA has the best cafeteria in the history of time," Nicky is sent to the waiting area so Dr. Silver can dig a bit deeper with us.

He sits with a clipboard and rattles off as many questions as the IEP forms we just filled out. Some of his inquiries overlap, but many are new and related to me and my health. While I know all the questions are meant to give the doctor a better picture of Nicky, it feels a bit like an interrogation. I half expect a flashlight and a set of handcuffs while the truth is pounded out of me.

"Have you or anyone in your family ever been diagnosed with a mental disorder?" Dr. Silver asks.

"I'm, um, on a little bit of Zoloft for anxiety. My dad had bipolar disorder. One of my sisters suffers from some pretty bad depression. Rex suffers from WASP Syndrome – the condition that forces one to look beautiful, white, wealthy and implode silently."

My attempt at humor does not go over well. Rex rolls his eyes while the doctor just plows ahead.

"How long exactly was your pregnancy?" he asks me.

I shift in my seat and try to remember exactly how many weeks early Nicky was born.

"He arrived five and a half weeks before my due date," I answer.

I study Dr. Silver's face, attempting to catch an expression of alarm or surprise – like perhaps Nicky's premature entrance to our world was the missing link to his Tourette's.

Nothing.

His face is frozen as stone. So much so, I'm tempted to call him Dr. Stone.

Furthermore, he's so mellow, I also consider calling him Dr. Stoner. With his gray shaggy hair, monotone vocals and robotic gestures, it's not hard to picture this world-famous psychiatrist lighting up before his rounds. It would sure make the one-hour intake more entertaining.

Dude, was it a C-Section or a vaginal birth? Like, how old was Nicky when he started talking? When did he chow down on

*his first vittles or get stoked on block building? I bet that was
totally tubular.*

No such luck. Dr. Silver is the epitome of a psychiatrist –
all business and emotionless fact digging. No question about
our son's physical, psychological, emotional and intellectual
development is left unasked. If our responses were put into a
time capsule and found ten thousand years from now,
scientists would no doubt be able to recreate an exact replica
of a nine-year-old boy.

I am bursting at the seams with a million questions for
the good doc, but I do my best to follow protocol and let him do
the talking for now. How can I get my son help if I don't give
the doctor all the basic information he needs? That would be
akin to talking to a high-end architect about the paint and roof
for my villa while he's just trying to get coordinates for the blue
print.

Taking off my mama bear hat for the time being, I put on
my logical fedora. I remind myself that this doctor evaluates
kids like Nicky every day. He travels the world as a keynote
speaker on Tourette Syndrome. He has more grants for his
clinical trials than my son has tics.

"Sometimes you just need to stay quiet and let the
professionals do their jobs," Glinda announces, putting a fuzzy
pink muzzle over my mouth. It matches my fedora and is made
from the softest velvet cotton blend.

"I'm not the patient type," I try to protest. But I can't.
She's got that gag on me tight. Perhaps if I'm quiet, Dr. Silver
will suggest a medication or a therapy that can gag some of my
kid's tics. Perhaps a muzzle in his favorite shade of blue.

"I'm sure you're interested in the types of therapies I
can offer your child," Dr. Silver says.

I shrug, doing my best to feign nonchalance when I
really want to jump up and scream, "Finally! BRING IT ON!"

"Before I can do that, I'd like to meet with Nicky alone," Dr. Silver says, putting down his clipboard. "It'll give me a chance to observe him and ask him some questions he might not feel comfortable answering with his parents in the room."

Translation: Overbearing parents can now exit the building.

"No problem." I am chipper and compliant. I pick up my purse and follow Rex out the door as Dr. Silver continues talking.

"Some kids tend to be a bit shy," Dr. Silver says, eyeballing Nicky down the hall. "So don't be surprised if it takes us longer than you might expect."

Before he has the opportunity to direct Nicky back to his office, Nicky jumps up from the couch and gets within two feet of Dr. Silver's granite face.

"What's up, Doc?" Nicky declares in his best Bugs Bunny expression. He points to the secretary, "That nice lady told me that she likes Mario a lot and I do, too, but my parents won't let me play it much. Mama says it will rot my brain cells and I think I'm doing just fine so . . . you know . . . can we talk about it?"

Dr. Silver pauses for a moment. He appears to stretch, but I'm pretty sure he uses that time to press an invisible button that triggers a protective force field between him and my overzealous child.

"We'll certainly talk about that, Nicky," he says. "Why don't you come this way?"

His final instructions are completely unnecessary as Nicky has already brushed past him, run through the door, and sprawled out comfortably on the couch.

"Ooh, very squishy!" Nicky remarks, running his hands over the pillows.

As Dr. Silver closes the door, the last words I hear are

Nicky's. "Can I take off my Crocs?"

I give Rex my best *that doc has no idea what he is in for* smirk.

"I know." Rex nods. "Our poor 'shy' child."

"What do you think so far?" I ask Rex who, as usual, fires up his I-phone to get some work done.

Our conversation goes like so many of our conversations of late. He remains a wall of pragmatic cement while I am a machine gun of emotion, trying to gun down his artfully erected partition.

Me: "So what do you think of Dr. Silver?"

Him: "He seems fine."

Me: "Aren't you glad we're finally getting some clarity?"

Him: "We haven't really gotten it yet."

Me: "I know, but we will. Very soon. Doesn't that feel like a relief?"

Him: "I'm relieved that you are going to be relieved."

Me: "Do you think he knows what he's talking about?"

Him: "I don't know, he hasn't really offered any suggestions yet."

Me: "But *based* on what you saw, do you think he will know what he's talking about?"

This is where Rex just stops talking. No worries. I just talk for him. In the process I also win an entry in the *Guinness Book of World Records* for Longest Run-On Sentence.

Me: "Let me guess . . . this is where you want to tell me that you can't predict Tourette's and you can't predict what strangers are going to say but you can predict that even if I tell you I'm finally going to have a game plan for Nicky's issues, the truth is that really I'm going to go round and round for the rest of our lives."

With this, Rex picks up his I-phone.

"Can you just record that for posterity?" He presses a

button. "Okay... go!" He points the gadget at my face

Channeling my inner Dr. Silver, I speak into the mouthpiece – nice and slow. "You. Are. The. Most. Annoying. Man. Alive."

Rex presses a button on his I-phone and then aims it my way. I hear my own words speak back to me, but instead of sounding flat and measured, they sound like a hyper Minnie Mouse on helium: "*YouAreTheMostAnnoyingManAlive!*"

I bust up laughing. The secretary shoots us a puzzled look before going back to her phone call.

"I love you," Rex says, taking my hand. "You know that, right?"

"I totally do," I say, grabbing his I-phone and pressing buttons on the screen.

"Watcha doing?" he says.

"Just looking for a cure for T.S.. Do you think there's an App for that?"

"Give that back to me," he says, putting his I-phone in his pocket. "We'll figure this out."

I'm not sure if Rex is referring to us or the tics or maybe both, but I don't care. It feels good to smile and just be together. For the next ten minutes Rex goes back to his work while I enjoy the feel of his hand in mine. It is large and strong. It makes me feel safe. I don't remember the last time I could say that.

And then it hits me. This is the first time – in forever – that we've done something truly intimate together. If it has to be in a shabby waiting room at UCLA, so be it.

I recall a meeting with Sam a few weeks back that touched on this very point. We had been discussing the effects of *Twitch and Bitch* on my mood.

"It's weird," I informed Sam. "It's not like anything has really changed in any of our lives, but it just feels better. I feel connected. Other women have said the same thing."

"That's the nature of intimacy," Sam said. "In fact, the word 'intimacy' when translated literally means *into me see.*"

I let Sam's words sink into my brain. They made sense – like water for a thirsty soul. Luckily for me, Sam opened up the hose and drenched me good.

"When you let people see you . . . the real you . . . it's freeing. It's scary at first, and it takes a lot of work and trust and courage, but if you can get past the initial hump, the magic happens."

His eyes sparkled. A true teacher, he knew my brain was finally starting to click and he ran with it. "When you feel free to be yourself, instead of isolating yourself in a funk — like you were before you stepped into this office — you feel more able to connect to others."

My head started to spin. "It's just so simple!" I retorted in a fake infomercial voice.

"Actually, it is," Sam replied with no hint of joking. "Instead of running around all over the place with your crazy emotions and thoughts, *Twitch and Bitch* has forced you to sit still and bond with others."

"If you call bitching bonding," I said.

"Normally I'd say no," Sam continued, "But in the case of your group, it's more like *bitching transformed* because you are venting with the attempt to find a solution – not just for the tics – but for how to handle them more rationally. That's a truth that resonates with people who want to be healthy. God didn't design us for a life of separation, but instead for fellowship. Fellowship equals connection. Connection equals healing."

"Which creates intimacy," I sighed, really grasping his point.

Sam nodded his head. For him, this concept was as natural as falling asleep after a long day. For me, it was revolutionary.

Relationship is something I had always done naturally as a child and young adult, but somewhere in my mothering and marriage – when I was forced to get behind the wheel rather than being a passenger – I had somehow lost my driving skills.

Sam's advice offered me the key to a brand new car... a chance to maneuver down a different road with intention. My mind was on fire with the possibility of the road trips my emotional life would take – and how nice it would be to have like-minded passengers on board.

"It's like meditation," I exclaimed. "I'll have to work on it every day, and really make it a practice. But once I start — like I did with *Twitch and Bitch* — my brain will feel peaceful. And, in feeling peace, I will feel more rested. And in feeling rested, I will feel more open to new ideas and transformation."

"Wash, rinse, and repeat," Sam said. "You keep going on like that and you'll find yourself more grounded than ever."

Sitting there in the UCLA waiting room, I know Sam was right. I know I've made some mistakes. But in an unconventional moment of clarity, it feels possibly . . . ever so slightly . . . that everything's going to be okay if I can just hold on.

Seconds later, Nicky comes bounding out before Dr. Silver. He runs down the hall and jumps on my lap.

"Mama! Papa! Doctor Silver says that video games are totally fine!" he shouts with glee.

I look up at Doctor Silver who, for the first time that day, is grinning ear to ear.

"Your son is a real character," Dr. Silver says. He continues to beam as he flashes a picture of Mario that Nicky had drawn for him in the office. The caption reads: "I make Nicky's brain bigger, not smaller! Mama is W-R-O-N-G!"

I'm glad to see some merriment in the otherwise stark physician, but I'm a bit surprised at his relaxed view of video gaming.

"It's time," Glinda says. And with that, she takes a sharp pair of sparkling scissors and cuts the muzzle off my mouth.

I can barely contain myself.

"Assuming what Nicky just said is true, I'm a little surprised that you'd be okay with his computer playing," I say.

Dr. Silver's once radiant smile reverts back to a flat-lipped smile. "What, specifically, surprises you?"

"Well, a lot of evidence supports that the neurotransmitters of the brain can get a little wonky from video game playing. Do you not agree with this?"

I can see the PhD Harvard-educated physician's brain melting at my choice word of 'wonky'. He responds, "The research of video games on children is wide and varied. Some studies show that it helps kids focus more. Others say it's less about screen time and more about the food they eat and their environment."

"That's another thing we need to talk about," I say. "What exactly is your stance on food and diet and how it affects tics and behavior?"

Dr. Silver just stares, apparently processing my questions with intent, so I continue.

"And what about alternative programs other than medicine that can affect a child's performance in school? I don't want my kid hyped up on crack nutrition and Mario games just to have him mellowed out by psychotropic drugs."

"I can see your point," Dr. Silver says. Before he can add anything, I say, "Good. Because I'm open to your suggestions, but I really want to pursue natural and obvious resources first before we go straight to medication."

Dr. Silver's expression remains blank. I'm quite certain

what he wants to say is, "If you want to pursue everything natural why did you haul your kid's butt to a doctor of psychiatry?" But instead just says, "Why don't we talk about this in my office?"

And so we do.

For the next forty-five minutes, we play verbal tennis.

When I bring up the gluten free/casein free diet, he reminds me that there isn't enough evidence to support it.

When I bring up rewiring a child's brain through alternative learning programs and biofeedback, he reminds me that there isn't enough research to back it up.

When I bring up my concern that maybe my kid is gifted *and not just because I'm that mother* and this is why his teachers don't seem to understand him, he reminds me that unless we have Nicky tested, we won't have a definitive answer.

I ask him what it will take to get the accurate evidence on all three counts. He tells me that he can't really speak to the nutrition or the brain rewiring options, but we can get Nicky tested through a private party for giftedness and an accurate diagnosis.

"How much will that cost us?" I ask.

"About two thousand dollars," he says.

"We don't have enough evidence . . . ahem . . . funds to support that," Rex pipes in.

"So what's next?" I ask the doctor.

Doctor Silver picks up his clipboard. "Well, I took a lot of notes. Seems to me that the three main concerns you have, in order, are:

1. What can we do for the tics?
2. What can we do for the impulse control?
3. What can we do for his focus?"

Yes. We were finally getting somewhere. We're going to

squash those little noises and I'll finally get some peace.

"But I would have to put number one, tic control, at the bottom of the list."

Damn! No such luck.

"On a scale of one to ten with Tourette's, ten being the most severe, I'd give Nicky a three. It's noticeable, but he's happy and content. He actually told me he likes his tics. Is this true?"

I want to scream, "That brat is lying." Instead I say, "It's true." I hope I don't sound as defeated as I feel.

"Well that's just . . . amazing," the doctor says. "I see kids all the time whose tics are affecting their emotional and social growth. That isn't the case with Nicky."

He goes on to add, "More important is his focus. If we can get that squared away, he'll control his impulses more, and in controlling his impulses, his tics might lessen."

This is where Rex gives his second contribution of the day. It is longwinded and I'm not sure I can digest his extremely wordy inquiry.

"How?"

"Well, we're currently doing a research trial at UCLA. It's a blind study that gives half the kids a placebo and half the kids Intuniv, a focus medication. Copious notes are taken, weekly questionnaires are sent home with you and to the school, and Nicky's health will be closely monitored by doctors. Assuming he gets the actual drug and not the placebo, it's an excellent way to see progress in small steps and get a better diagnosis for your son."

"What exactly is the purpose of the trial?" I ask.

"We are looking to see if Intuniv, which already works on kids with attention problems, also works for children with Asperger traits."

Here we go again. "Asperger traits? He has never even

been diagnosed. Are you saying he has this?"

"I've only seen him for twenty minutes, so it's hard to say. I've seen enough, though, to know that he fits the characteristics enough to get him into the study."

"Such as?" I say.

"For one, his fixation on a specific topic. In his case, video games. For another, his lack of coordination. For another, his inability to have a two-way conversation. Everything relates back to him."

"He's nine!" I say. "All kids that are nine are self-focused. As far as the other stuff, no one in our family plays sports. And yeah, he likes video games. My kid also fits the description of someone with ADD."

"No doubt. I see ADD in him big time."

At this moment I am more than happy to have a Catholic background firmly anchored in the Trinity, because in one minute this doctor has thrown out such a trifecta of labels it's going to take the Father, Son and Holy Ghost to keep me from needing an exorcism.

"Maybe some Intuniv will keep your head from spinning," interjects Rhonda. She downs an entire bottle of pills and falls flat to the floor.

Dr. Silver does his best to save the conversation," I have really no idea exactly what your son's diagnosis is. I can only speak to what I've read from his school reports and what I've observed today. I'm just offering one of many solutions."

"How much exactly will this trial cost?" Rex eyeballs the doctor cynically.

"It's free," Dr. Stone responds.

"We're in," I say, positive Rex will love this sound of 'free.'

"Not so fast," Rex interjects.

And so, my spring and summer from hell begins.

Takeways & Tips

- Go to your psychiatrist appointment calm and collected.
- Bring a list of questions to ask the doctor.
- Listen before you speak.
- Don't be afraid to ask questions afterwards.
- Don't expect your partner to think along the same lines as you. He might be wrong, but he might be right.
- If life is feeling particularly heavy, lighten it up! Have some fun! If you can't, find a friend that will force you to do it. Your husband and kids will thank you.
- If you have to choose between two medical facilities, choose the one with the best cafeteria. Bonus points if they serve Starbucks.

Chapter 17
TheoreTICal

"You must train your intuition. You must trust the small voice inside which tells you exactly what to say, what to decide."
~ Ingrid Bergman

When I enrolled my son in a clinical trial, I knew we'd be spending a lot of time both on the road as well as in waiting rooms. Rather than treat it like a weekly headache, I treated it like an adventure. Where would we go to lunch? How many quarters would we need for the parking meters? Would the therapy dog from the dementia building be there again this week and if so, would the owner mind if we brought it a treat?

I'm no perfect parent, but deep in my gut I knew that attitude would make all the difference in these long excursions as well as in the trial outcome itself. Looking back, I have wonderful memories of walking hand in hand with my son past university fountains. It was the first time he took an elevator by himself. It was his first experience in a college gift shop. My kid will likely not remember he even took part in a medication trial, but he'll hopefully remember that his mom and he had a lot of laughs – as well as a lot of ice-cream. It was HOT that summer. To this day, I can't eat a bowl of Dippin' Dots without thinking of Dr. Silver.

Ice cream and Aspergers – why not? I'll take the Double Scoop!

It's one pm on a Thursday. I am sitting in yet another dilapidated waiting room with Nicky. The sign outside the door reads "UCLA ADHD and Autism Clinic." Another mother sits across from me while her son plays on the X-box provided.

"Mama, why can't I play on the X-box also?" Nicky asks, looking up from the racetrack he's playing with.

"Because I actually want you to grow up with something called IMAGINATION rather than being a brainless, knuckle-dragging caveman automaton."

I speak low. I don't want to offend the mom sitting there, but she's too immersed in her own world. She doesn't even give me eye contact.

"Maybe she has Aspergers," Rhonda chimes in, gleefully.

"Maybe she's just as tired as you are," Glinda points out.

"Maybe you're both right," I say, trying to flip through a magazine. I really don't know what to think anymore.

I think back to two weeks ago. After leaving our Dr. Silver's, Rex and I hit two hours' worth of traffic. We used the time wisely. Nicky took photographs of telephone poles, freeway signs, the back of my head and the inside of his nostrils with my digital camera. Rex and I argued heatedly over doing this trial.

"It's free," I moaned. "I thought you'd be doing cartwheels. What's the problem?"

"It's not free," he countered. "Between gas, time, wear and tear on the car, and your sanity, it's going to cost us a fortune."

He wasn't wrong. Driving back and forth to UCLA every week with a ticking fourth grader all by my lonesome is not my idea of a funfest, but sitting home and stewing about a missed opportunity isn't an amazing option either.

All I can do is trust my gut and a burgeoning faith that tells me that where I am in my life is no accident and that everything will be fine.

With uncertainty swirling like a whirlpool, I don't know how I can remain so certain, but somehow I know if I just give in to the madness, rather than panicking and losing my breath, eventually I'll pop up further downstream.

To center myself for our first clinical trial meeting, I picture floating up a river. Whirlpools of credit card debt and twitches threaten to take me down on every side, but I am safe and secure in my puffy black inner tube.

Instead of pine trees on the shore, I see various versions of my fantasy future: My sparkling clean home, my handsome husband waving me over with a cup of Starbucks coffee, my daughter doing cartwheels, and my son gleefully singing "When I Meet the Wizard" from the musical *Wicked.*

"Show tunes? Why do you have to make him so gay?" Rhonda snorts, paddling by with a bright red helmet and a sleek yellow canoe.

"It's my fantasy," I retort, ignoring her jibes. "And I love that song!"

I really do. In it, Elphaba — tired of being judged for her green skin — dreams about meeting the wizard. She is convinced that her guru holds the keys to her ultimate happiness.

I can't help but think of Tourette's and how, maybe, just maybe, Dr. Silver is the silver bullet — the *wizard* — I've waited for. I've worked so hard! I've been so earnest! Maybe today my dreams will come true.

"Oh Heavens to Betsy with Whip cream and sparkles they *will*!" chirps Glinda, who plows over Rhonda with a monstrous pink shimmery motorboat. She throws me a life raft and pulls me up on deck by a glass elevator. Before one water drop hits the shining planks she snaps a finger and boom – My wet soaking clothes are transformed into an elegant pantsuit. The sky lowers to a dim black – the moon acting as my spot light – and the music starts up.

"Sing it, sister!" she squeals, shoving a powder pink

microphone in my face.

So sing I do.

"This is for my son," I whisper in my best smoky femme fatale voice, just before I start.

Did that really just happen?
Have I actually understood?
This weird quirk I've tried
To suppress or hide
Is a talent that could
Help me meet the wizard
If I make good
So I'll make good

The shoreline has transformed into an audience of fans, urging me to continue.

Once I'm with the wizard
My whole life will change
'Cuz once you're with the wizard
No one thinks you're strange!
No father is not proud of you,
No sister acts ashamed
And all of Oz has to love you
When by the wizard, you're acclaimed...

I give special emphasis to these last lyrics

And this gift or this curse
I have inside
Maybe at last, I'll know why
When we are hand in hand -
The wizard and I!

"Mrs. Frazer, the wizard will see you now." A research doctor in a dramatic fur-lined coat bows and waves me into the brightly lit corridor.

Actually, she's wearing a simple lab coat and states, "The doctor will see you now," in a flat monotone, but my version is much more exciting.

She asks me with a few specific questions about Nicky's health. It's then that I have a sudden flash of reality: The wizard never does cure Elphaba's external condition.

It's a sobering thought that anchors me back to reality. With what's about to unfold over the next six weeks, being grounded is a good place to be.

***

Halfway down the hall we run into Dr. Silver. After taking Nicky's chart from the research doctor, he walks us the rest of the way to the conference room.

"Are dogs allowed?" Nicky asks, dangling his well-worn Snoopy by the collar.

"I suppose we can make the exception," Dr. Silver says with faux seriousness. "Does he bite?"

"No, but he does give kisses," Nicky warns. "He likes people."

"You seem to like people, too," Dr. Silver says.

"I do," Nicky beams.

"Then you're going to love a program we have here at UCLA called Circle of Friends. I'll tell you all about it once we're seated."

Dr. Silver leads us into a barren meeting space. The outside of it is framed in cement. I get the impression an architect who loved Star Trek engineered the design.

The inside of the space craft/conference room is one long table, chairs and more cement walls. It's austere to say the least. Perhaps its barrenness is to better focus on the people. With Nicky's curly hair, world worn Snoopy, bright blue Mario shirt, and snack bag, it would take a blind person not to pay attention to this kid.

"Can we eat in this place?" Nicky asks, after first settling himself in a chair and setting his pet next to him.

"I don't see why not," Dr. Silver answers. "Didn't you eat at the cafeteria?" he asks, a witty nod to Nicky's favorite place on earth.

"I am going to eat there afterwards," Nicky says. "I could live there, it's so delicious." His focus shifts as he thrusts his hand into a plastic bag. "Want a pistachio?"

"Why not?" Dr. Silver agrees.

Nicky takes a few and rolls them across the table like a professional craps dealer shooting dice.

"Good shot!" Dr. Silver says. "Why don't you play sports? You're quite good."

"I don't like them," Nicky says.

"Ah," Dr. Silver shakes his head with empathy. He looks over his notes.

"Is it because other kids won't let you play with them?"

"It's not that," Nicky says, "But I'm sometimes the last picked for hand ball in P.E."

"Oh, that must make you feel sad," Dr. Silver clucks.

"Not really," Nicky says, making a happy face out of pistachio shells on the faux oak conference table. "I don't mind."

"Really, Nicky?" Dr. Silver's voice is calm and encouraging. "How can being picked last feel okay?"

"I like it because I can see the patterns of all the kids and how they hit the ball. By the time I get into the square, I know exactly what to expect. Those suckers are doomed when Super Nicky arrives on the scene!"

Dr. Silver smiles. "You're pretty smart."

"I know," says Nicky, "My mom says that's why I tic."

"I see," says Dr. Silver. "And does that ever make you feel different?"

"Yes," says Nicky, his voice low as if subconsciously attempting to match Dr. Silver's tone.

"What's it like to feel different?" Dr. Silver continues.

"I love it!" Nicky says, bright smile on his face. "It's what makes me special."

"You certainly are special, Nicky," Dr. Silver says, "which leads me back again to that program I mentioned – Circle of Friends."

"What's that? Do friends sit around a circle like in circle time and sing songs and stuff? Because that's kind of a kindergarten thing and I'm in fourth grade."

"Oh, it's not *that* babyish, Nicky," Dr. Silver says, waving away such foolish thoughts, "It's for kids just like you – kids who might sometimes have a rough time making friends."

"I don't have a rough time making friends." Nicky is aghast at the thought. "I have *lots* of boys and girls I hang out with!"

Dr. Silver shoots me a quizzical look. I nod in agreement at Nicky's last statement.

"Well, in this group you can make new friends. There's someone called a counselor who runs it, and he will teach you how to chat with other kids in an appropriate way."

"I already know how to talk appropriately. In fact, I sometimes talk sooo much I'm sent outside the classroom where there's no way I can bother all the friends in my class."

"You don't have to join if you don't want," the doctor says, "but it's an option. In fact, the reason you're here today is because we're not sure if you, like a whole lot of other kids that I see, have something called Aspergers."

"*Ass* burgers?" Nicky laughs out loud. "I might have *Butts in Bread*? That is very inappropriate! You need to join Circle of Friends!"

Dr. Silver chuckles and continues. "All it means to have Aspergers is that your brain works a little differently than some of the other kids in your class. For example, you think about certain topics a lot— "

"Like video games!" Nicky jumps in.

"Yes, like that. Or perhaps you don't always give eye contact."

Nicky delivers his best laser-like gaze at the doctor and holds it, as if daring him to join him in an impromptu staring contest. Dr. Silver declines the challenge and instead sticks to the topic at hand.

"Some other signs of Aspergers are being very stuck on certain routines or taking everything that is said literally – meaning, word for word. By coming to my office, every week for eight weeks, we will give you little tests along with some medication to get a better picture of whether you have this or not. Also, the medication, called Intuniv, will calm you down so you can focus more in class."

"Forget it. I'm not taking medication," Nicky hugs Snoopy closer.

"But Nicky, it won't only help you pay better attention. It will also calm down your tics."

"How many times do I have to tell you – *I LIKE MY TICS!*"

Dr. Silver sighs. If a thought bubble could appear over his head at this moment, it would read: "Incorrigible Punk." He plows ahead anyway.

"My research assistant already discussed this with your mother. I'm running a blind trial, which basically means you might get Intuniv, or you might just get a placebo which is another word for "sugar pill."

"The sugar pill will make my tics even stronger, you know," Nicky scoffs.

"Well that would work out well for you, wouldn't it, since you love them so much?" Dr. Silver points out.

Nicky's eyes are closed. His arms are folded across his chest. He's not budging or calling the doctor's bluff.

"I don't care what you say. I am not taking any pills, sugar or not. Nothing you can say or do will get me to shove those things down my mouth.

"UCLA is paying me twenty five dollars a visit to cover parking and gas," I step in. "How about instead of keeping it for myself I give it to you each week as a present for trying the medication?"

"Works for me!" Nicky shouts, holding out his hands for quick cash.

And just like Esau who sold his birthright for a bowl of lentils, my moneygrubber was officially ready to embark down Pharmaceutical Highway.

***

For the next three weeks I faithfully give Nicky his pill every morning. I also give his teacher paperwork from UCLA to track his performance in class. Week after week I receive word that that not only has his focus not improved, it's actually gotten worse.

His tics, as fate would have it, have also severely increased, which means my anxiety level skyrockets. I don't dare say anything to my husband lest I get an "I told you so" UCLA tirade, but I give an earful to the research assistant, Adina.

"His tics are worse than I've ever seen them," I say to her after Nicky goes back to the waiting room to pretend to play with a race track when, in reality, he's obsessing over kids playing video games in front of him. "I know I said that when we started the program one month ago, but now I really mean it."

"Well, for the record, his vocal tics didn't keep him from giving me a ten minute play by play of his latest adventure with the Mario Wii. He is so adorable!"

Adina smiles, all red hair and freckles. She is warm and genuine and truly thinks my kid is the cat's meow. Given how sterile Stink's doctor is, I appreciate this research assistant's warmth. But right now, I'm not interested in compliments. I'm interested in answers. And I'm going to get one.

"The doctor said that Intuniv lowers tics as well as blood pressure," I say. "Given that he's been running like a jack rabbit with turpentine up its rear, I'm guessing he's been given the placebo."

She looks over Nicky's chart. "His vitals have remained the same over the past few weeks," she says. "I can't say for sure... and you didn't hear this from me... but I think your hunch is dead on."

"Can't we end this trial early?" I plead. "I'm dying."

My voice is cracking. It's as if the world is playing some cosmic joke on me. I am starting to slowly accept that I'm not going to magically fix the tics, but I certainly don't want to make them worse.

"We can't," she sighs in empathy. "In order for the trial to be considered valid, we have to do the entire run."

"We also wouldn't want the good doctor to not get his kickback from the pharmaceutical company that is likely sponsoring this big investigation either," I say, my emotions switching from desperation to aggravation.

"For what it's worth," Adina confides, "I hear you one hundred percent. Everything is run so clinically – to the point where sometimes the kid gets lost in the process."

"You can say that again," I nod. "I had to sell my soul to

get an appointment in the first place, and before I know it, I'm paying off my kid to take drugs that may or not be working for a condition that he may or may not have. How did I go from definite Tourette's to possible Aspergers? And when will I know for sure?"

"Well, to get him diagnosed with Aspergers, you'll have to go through a private clinician. It could cost about two thousand dollars."

"Are you serious?" I sputter. "Dr. Silver said that by doing this trial I'd have a good idea – due to all your exams and intakes – about Nicky's diagnosis.

"Well, yeah, you'd have an *idea*," she said, flipping through the stack of papers, "But it's not the same as a clinical definition that you'd need for school purposes. Our research is not going to get your kid an IEP or special classroom accommodations such as 504 down the road."

If I could cry, I would. My emotional balloon is too deflated. I settle instead for a string of truth.

"Level with me, Adina," I'm sitting straight as a soldier, looking right into her hazel eyes. They are warm and kind. I trust her. "Does my kid have Aspergers?"

"It's hard to say," she replies, not breaking my gaze.

I audibly sigh as I slump back in my chair. Now the tears start to come. Adina is not flustered. She hands me a tissue and continues.

"He *does* fit some of the characteristics – enough to make him qualify for this Aspergers/Intuniv trial - but he doesn't fit all of them. It's difficult to say whether he's on the spectrum or just super eccentric.

"Excellent. When shall I expect the official paperwork from UCLA stating that my kid is certifiably strange?"

She laughs. "Well, his mother isn't exactly average. He's strange in a good way. He's his own person. Look at all those artists out there making their mark on the world. They didn't get there by fitting into a neat little box. Look at Steve Jobs!"

"He turned out great," I grunt, "But what about his poor mother?"

"What about her?" Adina asks, handing me another tissue.

"Everyone talks about how Steve Job's eccentricity changed the world – which is awesome – but can you even imagine raising that kid? How did his mother survive it? He must have been hell on wheels."

"Maybe," she sympathizes, "But I bet at some point she also realized that her son was going to forge his own path, no matter how much hair she yanked from her head."

She has a point, of course. In addition to wishing I could sit down over a glass of wine with Steve Job's mom, I couldn't help but think of my favorite Steve Jobs quote:

Here's to the crazy ones, the misfits, the rebels, the troublemakers, the round pegs in the square holes . . . the ones who see things differently -- they're not fond of rules . . . You can quote them, disagree with them, glorify or vilify them, but the only thing you can't do is ignore them because they change things . . . they push the human race forward, and while some may see them as the crazy ones, we see genius, because the ones who are crazy enough to think that they can change the world, are the ones who do.

"Look, Adina, I'm not saying you're wrong about any of this. In fact, I'm quite certain that because of me – *in spite of me* – my quirky little maybe–on–the–spectrum–maybe–not–ADD–ticker will blossom into a crazy successful adult. But right now, he's in fourth grade and I've got to raise him. And this mad ticking needs to stop. NOW."

"So, you want out of the trial?" Adina puts down her folder.

"Not quite. I first want to put my placebo question to rest. I'm pretty sure this is what is causing his upswing in tics. Did you hear back from the doctor on that?"

"Oh, yes . . . I spoke to him this morning. He says it's impossible for a kid to be allergic to a placebo. He said the increase is likely due to state testing or his recent bout of strep."

"Of course that's what he said," I say, rolling my eyes. "Well, Adina, I'm going to have to respectfully disagree." I start packing up my purse. "Let's see how things stand this time next week."

"I think giving it another week is a wise idea," Adina says, looking up at me. She hesitates a moment before adding, "I might not be here next Thursday. This place . . . the way it focuses on the mind but not the soul . . . it's not for me."

I look at her but don't say a word. This time, it's *her* eyes that well up. I pass her a tissue and instinctively reach over the desk and hug her. I'm like a six foot one giant pretzel hunched over her waif-like frame.

"You'll be missed," I say as I let go of the embrace. I know, without having to ask her, that this will be the last time we will speak. I subconsciously understand that working on a UCLA trial, the Mafia, and the Boy Scouts all have the same motto: "Leave no trace."

Her parting words to me are all I need to hear. "Whatever you decide, Andrea, you know best."

***

With her words still ringing in my ears, I sign off on another week of UCLA medication.

On the way to the cafeteria, I hand Nicky his twenty five dollars for swallowing his pills each morning, even though I already know, without a shadow of doubt, that I'll be dumping the new batch down the toilet that evening.

The next morning, I tell Nicky his pill has been crushed in his food – a blatant lie, but needed. I don't trust my little do-gooder not to sell me down the river to Dr. Silver if he knows I am cheating.

By afternoon, despite the "pressures of state testing" still going on and a head cold, his tics are reduced by half. By our next appointment with UCLA, the tics are almost gone.

"I told you he wasn't allergic to the medication!" Dr. Silver ribs me.

"You were a hundred percent right," I concede, fingers behind my back and three Hail Mary's for good luck.

I need to keep up my lie for two more weeks. I pray if I die I don't end up in hell, but then I comfort myself with the knowledge that I'm already in it.

***

Two weeks later I am seated across from Dr. Silver. It's the day of the big reveal. I kick myself for not wearing a ball gown. If only, instead of sitting across from this gray-haired psychiatrist, I was sitting in an audience staring at Hugh Jackman.

Dr. Silver pulls a sheet of paper out of a gold envelope. *And the winner is...*

"Placebo!" he says, waving the certification letter for dramatic effect.

I feel like presenting this world renowned doctor with paperwork of my own from a similar gold envelope: "No kidding, Kojak!"

Instead I go with, "What happens next?"

"Next we go with the Intuniv," he says. "Just like before, we will compensate you for your time and monitor Nicky's reaction to the medication week by week."

"I have to think about it," I answer truthfully.

"I understand," he replies, "Talk it over with your husband and email us tomorrow. I'd really love to see if the medication makes a difference in Nicky's school performance."

Translation: I'd like to complete this trial in full so I can pay rent on my yacht in the Marina.

"I couldn't agree more," I say, "I'll get back to you within twenty four hours."

True to my word, I email Dr. Silver the next day.

Hi Dr. Silver –

After extensive thought about Nicky taking part of your Intuniv research study, we've decided to decline at this time.

In short, you were all awesome and so lovely to work with. We appreciate your time and expertise more than you know.

The reasons we're against the drugs at this time came down to the following main points:

· Nicky loves himself, tics and all (We don't want to drown out his joy and if he's okay with his tics, that's pretty darn impressive. What an advocate he will be for T.S.!)

·He focuses well enough. He's at the 95th percentile of the school district.

· He has loads of friends so he is not being impacted socially at this time, which is always a concern for Aspergers kids.

Speaking of Aspergers, if Nicky truly does have high functioning Aspergers, we'd like the paperwork on this so I'm clearer on the reasoning behind the diagnosis.

Maybe in a year or so if he is impacted either socially or academically that will change and we'd love to reconnect.

Until then, best on your project,

Andrea and Rex

Five minutes later I forward the email to Mr. Parker so he'd know what to expect the final two weeks of class. While I could be proud of myself for keeping his teacher in the loop at all times, I probably should have done a little editing first – particularly the P.S. of my email which read,

P.S. His teacher might be annoyed by him, but I'm not willing to drug up my child to make him more docile if he's not willing to engage him more on an intellectual level.

That didn't go over so well.

Takeways & Tips
- Don't be afraid to do a research trial, but be aware of what you're getting into so you know whefn to call it quits or move forward.
- If you decide to go with medication, ask as many questions as you want from the doctor. It's your child! And get a second opinion if you want.
- Listen to how your child feels so they feel heard, but at the end of the day, it's your decision whether to put your child on meds or not. You're the adult.
- Be careful who you confide in about medication vs. no medication, especially if your nerves are fragile. There are very strong opinions on both fronts and you deserve an objective opinion so you can make the decision
- Don't make any decisions based on fear.
- Be honest with your child's teachers, but not so honest that they want to send you to hell at the end of the school year.

- Don't drink merlot and email. It's bad for your reputation.

Chapter 18
ApologeTIC

"Before you can live a part of you has to die. You have to let go of what could have been, how you should have acted and what you wish you would have said differently. You have to accept that you can't change the past experiences, opinions of others at that moment in time or outcomes from their choices or yours. When you finally recognize that truth then you will understand the true meaning of forgiveness of yourself and others. From this point you will finally be free."
~ Shannon L. Adler

Often we can get so wrapped up in our thinking that we make rash decisions based on emotion. When that happens, we can live in regret and anger and bitterness or we can do the one simple thing that's hardest of all – we can say, "I'm sorry."

For many of us, this concept might feel completely unfair, especially when we feel other people should apologize to us. But that's not how it works — especially when it comes to raising a kid with Tourette's or other special needs. It's not like our kid's diagnosis came with a manual: "When Tic X happens, react with Action Y . . . When Doctor-Know-It-All Suggests A, respond with Reaction B."

I learned that I could do my best to react appropriately or create a plan, but sometimes everything went to hell in a hand basket.

Translation: Mama said there'd be days like this.

When I lost my cool with a doctor, my spouse, an educator, my kid or even an unsuspecting tic-toc clock, at some point I stopped flogging myself for acting like a spoiled brat and started over with a simple apology. Despite my feelings of self-pity, anger or even despair, I had to accept life on life's terms and act maturely. I had to put on the big girl panties.

Maybe you need to start over? If so, here's your virtual underwear. It's got a lot of elastic, so you have no excuse not to stretch and breathe deeply. (Pssssst: They're oversized briefs. I've got your ass covered.)

PS: This is also part 1 of 2 God chapters. Don't freak out on me. But if you must, I'll just go with the theme of this chapter and say it upfront: "I'm Sorry."

"I'm so tired of apologizing to everyone," I tell Sam, feet up on his couch.

I'm wearing my Cookie Monster slippers. Not everyone would choose to wear giant blue Sesame Street sleepwear out of their house, let alone their therapist's office, but life is too short for formalities. It's been a hell of a week. After telling Mr. Parker I was sorry for slamming his teaching, then apologizing to UCLA for turning down their Intuniv Study only to change my mind a few days later and beg to get Nicky back in, I'm not apologizing about my choice in footwear.

"Why do I always have to make the first move? Why isn't everyone running around asking for *my* forgiveness?" I ask Sam.

"What would Cookie Monster say?" he says, eyes twinkling.

"He would say, 'I'm sorry these cookies aren't gluten free, but it's not going to cure your kid's tics anyway, so suck it."

Sam laughs. "So, you decided to opt back into the trial after all?"

"Yeah," I admit, taking a big sip of Diet Coke. "After thinking about entering a summer with twitches and hyperactivity, I decided it made sense to at least give it a shot. It's not a mind -altering drug. Worst case it doesn't work and we're back where we started. But at least I'll have closure."

"How's it going so far?" he says.

"So far so good," I say, truthfully. "His tics are almost gone. I mean, *gone*. Then again, he's so tired from adjusting to the medication, he doesn't have the energy to tic."

"How's Nicky dealing with it?" Sam asks.

"He doesn't love it," I admit, a bit wistfully. "Yesterday he came into my room and started sobbing. 'These pills are giving me so many mini-cries, Mama!'"

"I felt bad about it, but I told him we couldn't go through another year like fourth grade. We had to try something new."

"And he accepted that?" Sam looks doubtful.

"He begged me to go off of them," I sigh, "But I put my foot down. I told him if it continued in a week, we'd lower the dosage or find a different approach."

"You set the expectation, dealt with the emotional response, listened but stayed detached, then set a back-up plan. That seems reasonable," he says, going into his therapist-slash-coach mode. I half expect a screen to fall out of midair where he'll point to a chart replete with "x's," "o's" and lots of manic circles for emphasis.

"Not much else you can do," he finishes, arms crossed.

"What about crying and moaning in indecision?" I whimper.

"No way," he says. "You've gone too far with boundary setting for that. Congratulations. You have almost mastered the Codependence Course."

"Almost?"

"Well, there's still the little matter of your marriage," he says.

"Hey, I admit I am ... *was* ... codependent with the T.S.,

but I'm not codependent with Rex!" I am aghast at the notion.

At this, Sam's head jerks up so fast from his computer screen that I'm half attempted to diagnosis him with a tic or a demon.

"Are you joking?" he gasps.

I shrug my shoulders and solemnly stare at him. My bug-eyed character shoes notwithstanding, I'm the epitome of seriousness.

"What do you call all that stuff about fighting over the finances, or about your work/life balance?"

"I call that my spouse being rigid and controlling," I say, grasping at straws.

"I'm not saying how he *acts*," Sam says, "I'm talking about how *you* act when he doesn't do what you want," he says.

"I get mad and annoyed," I say.

"Why?" he asks.

"Because I care?"

"Try again."

"Because it pisses me off?"

"Try again."

"Because now *you're* pissing me off?"

"Because you're codependent!" he says, slapping his knee for emphasis. "Do you even know what that means?"

"Not really." I put on a pouty face. "I hope that doesn't make you mad at me because your response could make me feel really stupid and ruin my self-esteem."

"Joke away, but I am less codependent and more co-pay dependent."

I laugh at that. I swear, sometimes Sam is really worth every single penny.

"This is what I'm looking for," he says, pointing to his computer screen. He reads,

Codependency is a learned behavior that can be passed

down from one generation to another. It is an emotional and behavioral condition that affects an individual's ability to have a healthy, mutually satisfying relationship. It is also known as 'relationship addiction' because people with codependency often form or maintain relationships that are one-sided, emotionally destructive and/or abusive.

I am okay until that last sentence.

"Whoa, horsey. Rex is a pain, but he's not a wife batterer," I say, oddly protective of the man I so often complain about.

"I'm not saying he's abusive," he says, "But the feeling of having a one-sided relationship can feel that way from the receiving end."

This time it's my head that jerks up to look at Sam. Knowing he has my attention, he continues in earnest, "Your needs aren't being met by your husband. It's that simple."

Before I can interrupt him, he continues, "But that's okay, because it's not his job to make you happy. By the same token, it's not your job to make him happy. And yet, until you are able to understand this, you'll be doing the equivalent of forever emptying water from a boat with a hole in the floorboard. You know as well as I do what's gonna happen."

"The boat sinks," I say. "But what about Rex and me?"

"Oh, good news there," he says. "It's a happy ending."

"Thank God," I murmur, but before I can say anything else, he adds: "You die."

I don't know what to do other than cover my head with my hands to keep my melting brain from exploding out my ears. I am so flustered I can't speak. This is perfectly fine with Sam as today he's on fire.

"Raising a special needs kid isn't easy," he says. "A lot of marriages break up over it. But if you're willing to look at Tourette's as a gift instead of a burden, your marriage can be stronger than ever before, because it will have forced you both to do what you might not have done in the past."

"You mean kill each other?"

"No," he says. "You get to kill your egos, live life on life's terms and recreate yourselves as a new couple."

"How simple," I scoff.

"It's not easy," he says. "That's why so many people don't do it. It's impossible to do alone. That's where God comes in."

Here we go again with this God stuff. Couldn't there be an easier and softer path? Perhaps some Namastes, an enlightening Ted Talk and a crap load of doobage?

"At some point, Andrea, you're going to have to trust that something higher than yourself can bring your life to a whole new level. When you're willing to admit you don't have all the answers, you'll be able to truly die to self. In putting the old Andrea to death, you'll be reborn as a more grounded, more centered Andrea."

I don't say a word. I just listen. If shutting my pie hole is not a God-induced miracle I don't know what is.

"You can have a new life, Andrea. That's what the gospel promises," he says.

Ah, the New Testament stuff again. It always comes back to that, doesn't it? And yet, if it's such Good News, why do I feel like such garbage?

"I actually like what you have to say, Sam, but I'm still kind of uncomfortable with this whole Jesus thing," I admit. "I mean, it sounds like he set some pretty good boundaries in his day. But look what happened to him. They nailed him to a cross. I'm not really a crucifixion kind of girl," I say.

"Then stop being God, put your cross down, and accept that Jesus did that for you."

I'd like to argue with Sam on this one, but I can't. I'm too busy crying. I can't put my finger on why I'm so moved, but I know that something has shifted. I know that, despite this painful season of my life – or perhaps because of it – I'm going to be a better parent to my son as well as a better wife.

"Okay," I say, forming words from my heart instead of my head. "I'm going to trust you on this one. It's just . . . hard."

"The more you give it to God, the less painful it will be," Sam says. "Did you know an acronym for GOD is Grow or Die?"

"I do now," I say. "I just wish this growing could go a bit faster."

"You'll have to take it minute by minute, step by step," he says, winking.

Little do I know, that afternoon I'll be offered plenty of practice to walk. I'm just grateful that I have, by that time, switched from Cookie Monster slippers into tennis shoes.

Takeways & Tips

- When you're wrong, say you're sorry.
- Even if you don't think you're wrong, think about how you contributed to the situation that made you angry. If you really think about it, you'll probably find your part in it. Do as I suggested in the first place and friggin' apologize.
- Saying sorry doesn't mean what the other person, situation or thing did is okay. It means that you're taking responsibility for your response to it. (Translation: You acted like a baby and threw a tantrum. Time to grow up.)
- Consider that maybe you don't have all the answers and someone/something outside yourself does.
- When it comes to your relationships, remember that you don't always get to have your way,

but you can always speak your truth. In doing so, you'll feel more peaceful about not getting your way. (Bonus: More peace means less tantrums, which means less apologizing from you. Yay!)

Chapter 19
SpiritualisTIC

"Always forgive your enemies; nothing annoys them so
much."
~ Oscar Wilde

*I've heard it said that not forgiving someone is like
drinking a poison and expecting the other person to die. The only
one who suffers is you. And that's, well, stupid. Go ahead and
apologize to yourself for that one, okay? Maybe it's a person you
need to forgive. Maybe it's a disorder you never saw coming and
has played havoc on your or your child's emotions or body (or
yours). Whatever it is, it's time to drop the rock.*

*For me, taking a leap of faith was crucial in this process.
I'm not saying all of you want to drink the Jesus juice and go on a
pilgrimage to Our Blessed Lady of Tics and Twitches. But I am
suggesting, with all due respect, that giving it up to a power
greater than yourself can take that pressure off your shoulders.
(Not to mention that you'll tap into a whole new community of
like-minded people who are trying to transform pain into
meaning. Who knew tics could turn you into such a guru of
enlightenment?)*

It's hotter than Hades and there's not a stitch of food in
the house. To avoid starvation, Rex and I cobble together a plan
to take the children to lunch.

The kids are cranky. Rex and I are cranky. The car is
cranky and showing its protest to our lunch excursion by
blowing lukewarm air from the vents.

As we roll down the windows and sweat rolls from our faces, Nicky decides to bring up an issue he had at school.

"I forgot to tell you I was sent to the office on Friday," he tells me, kicking his legs into the back of Rex's seat.

"Stop that," Rex gripes, stretching his back in annoyance.

"What's the magic word?" Nicky pokes, both figuratively and literally. He kicks Rex's seat again.

"I'll give you three magic words: STOP. THAT. NOW." Rex huffs.

"Papa is right," I tell Nicky, "It's not nice. Now continue with what you were saying."

"I was sent to the office for running away from Mr. Parker." His voice is somber with a twinge of frustration.

"Why did you run away?" I ask.

"Because he wouldn't let me get the pistachios that spilled out of my bag after the bell rang."

The car breaks to a halt in a parking space, forcing us forward. Rex turns around and stares at Nicky, eyes lit with irritation.

"I told you to stop banging into my seat!"

"I forgot! I'm sorry!" Nicky whines.

I rub Rex's knee in, as much as I hate to admit it, a codependent attempt to diffuse a bomb. "He's just a kid who is trying to explain something important," I mutter.

"And I'm just the father who wants to find a parking space in peace! That's important, too!"

"I hear you," I say, trying my best not to laugh, "But it scares me when you drive like that. It's erratic and jarring and—"

"Oh give me a break," he cuts me off. "Nicky has no respect for how hard I work, how exhausted I am, how much money we are about to spend on lunch, and instead of disciplining him, you're on his side."

"I'm on your side, too— "

"Bullsxsx you are," he interrupts me again.

"He said bullsxsx," Nicky whispers over to Evie, who starts to giggle.

"Watch your language," I say, no longer seeing the humor in the situation.

"I hope Nicky's not on his way to that cursing side off T.S.," Rhonda chimes in from the reflection in the side view mirror. (I swear she shows up at the most inconvenient times.)

"I'm also really tired of being interrupted," I snipe, working in overdrive to keep my voice level. "It's a bad example for the kids and—"

"Just get out!" Rex screams at everyone.

His words hit like slaps. In record time we exit the vehicle, me propelled by anger, the kids propelled by hunger and drama. Rex and I walk ahead with the children madly galloping to keep up.

Nicky squeezes in between us and tugs on our arms for attention. "When Miss Kay asked why I ran away from Mr. Parker, I told her I was just frustrated from having to stand with Jenny under the sex cloud."

Both of us turn to our son. We are dumbstruck. Luckily our third grade daughter speaks for us.

"You told me Jules and Ricky made you sit under the *kissing* cloud!" Evie exclaims.

Nicky is incredulous. "It started out as that, but then they turned it into the sex cloud when I wouldn't hold Jenny's hand. I told Miss Kay that it was okay that my parents hold hands and have sex and everything, but I'm only in fourth grade and *that was very inappropriate!*"

We are now at the restaurant door.

I am bursting with frustration.

Rex responds with, "What do you want for lunch?"

The most gifted fortuneteller couldn't have predicted the words that would spill out of my mouth. I wanted to say "I'm sorry" for irritating him, but instead I find myself near shouting, "Our fourth grader is concerned about sex clouds and pistachios and all you can think about is tacos???"

"I actually want a burrito," Evie chimes in.

"Can I have a cheese quesadilla for once?" Nicky adds. "It's not gluten free but it would distract me from the nasty sex cloud—"

"No you cannot!" Rex interrupts him. "*I'm* ordering lunch so we can be back in thirty minutes because I have a lot of work I need to get done for Monday."

Rex opens the door to let us in, but we all just stand there — Nicky and Evie shooting pouty faces at their food censor, me staring at the ground. I don't want to ruin the day, but I'm not quite ready to go in and order the family taquito special. I take a deep breath, determined not to say something I don't mean. Or worse, say what I really think.

"If you could just go in with the kids, I'll be there in five minutes," I say, spotting a stone fountain nearby where I can sit and cool down.

"No." My husband's voice is cold and resigned.

"What?" I look up from the cement and stare into smoldering eyes.

"No," he says. "Either we go now as a family or we don't eat."

"What, you're my father now?" I ask, floored at his audacity to decide what we will and will not do.

"No. I'm just your husband who, apparently, can't do anything right. And so to avoid pissing you off or damaging our precious children any further, I'm just going to go."

He starts to leave. I call after him, "Oh come on! This is

ludicrous!"

He turns around. "I'll come back if you apologize."

Here's my chance! But I can't. Instead I respond, "For what?" I am beside myself in the madness of this conversation.

"That's what I figured."

He keeps walking. He doesn't turn around. I yell after him again.

"How are we supposed to get home? You have the car!"

He turns around, looks me squarely in the eye, and says, "Try walking."

And off he goes.

A million thoughts float through my mind as I attempt to gleam something positive to say to Rex at this moment. Something encouraging and kind. Something reminiscent of grace and forgiveness and mercy.

Instead I go with, "You're a schmuck!" screamed from the top of my lungs.

Nicky snickers and whispers to Evie, "She said schumck."

Two seconds later. "Mama, what's a schumuck?"

***

A million thoughts are running through my head as I walk hand in hand with my kids into the noisy fast food joint.

"My husband is a jerk."

"Was I too hard on him?"

"Are my kids going to be psychologically damaged from this terrible interchange?"

I'm vacillating between despair at the interchange and euphoria at standing up for myself. And yet, between the clanging symphonies of feelings fighting for performance time in the orchestra of my brain, one singular emotion sweeps over me: peace.

Quiet but assertive, unexpected serenity acts as a

soothing cloud cover over the heat of my jangled nerves. As I scan for empty booths, a small still voice can be heard beneath the cacophony of fellow customers and my emotions: *Pray*.

"So, what, you're hearing voices now?" Rhonda is dressed in spiked heels with devil's horns. Like my anger, she seems to have grown tenfold. She is leering over me with eyes of fire. But in those eyes, I sense something I had not seen before: *fear*.

Again, that word comes back in my head: *Pray*.

And so, before Rhonda can change my mind, I do.

Dear God, I begin, *Help me*.

"He will," says another voice. It's none other than Glinda's. She is dressed in a brown monk's robe. Birkenstocks cover unmanicured toes, a sharp departure from the usual garb of ball gowns and stilettos. But her makeup is exquisite and her hair is tucked under a silk cream scarf, so I know it's her.

"You've come as far as you can on your own," she says. "It's time to do what Sam said. Give it up to the Guy Upstairs. He has a plan for you, for the tics, for everything."

At that moment, I'm not sure if it's the hunger talking or I've simply lost my mind, but she makes a lot of sense. In fact, as I turn to Rhonda, I see that she's shrunk to half her size. When I look at her, she's really nothing more than that little sixth grade bully from my grammar school days, scowling in a devil's Halloween costume.

"I am not the Bible Thumper type," I tell Glinda, fearful she's going to slap me with the Good Book.

"Hot rollers, not holy rollers," she responds, taking off her scarf and letting her hair fall down from its curlers in long, cascading waves. "Just talk to Him. You won't have immediate answers, but you'll have a sense of calm to nudge you forward."

She reaches into her deep brown robes and pulls out a pink bedazzled NIV Bible. "But don't knock this sucker. It's a page-turner and you won't believe how it ends!"

And with that, she puts it back in her pocket, sweeps up what is left of Rhonda – nothing but a small red cape and a plastic horn and tail - and disappears.

With Rhonda's chatter out of my brain, I get the kids settled with crayons and activity placemats at a high café table. I cross my fingers that they won't fall off the bar stools and get in line to order food.

There's a long line of customers before me, but for once, I'm happy about the wait. It gives me a chance to collect my thoughts and to, well, pray.

I feel a bit awkward, not to mention insecure. But vulnerability with an upgrade is better than anger or depression, because it means, in reaching out to others, or in this case, God, I am rewarding myself with what every human being needs the most to thrive: connection.

As Brene Brown wrote in her book *Daring Greatly*, "Love and belonging are irreducible needs of all men, women and children. We're hard wired for connection – it's what gives purpose and meaning to our lives. The absence of love, belonging and connection always leads to suffering."

Citing "being dumped at a strip mall" as the primary reason, I'm at my breaking point with this suffering. It's time to try something different.

So I do.

Dear God,
I, um, I need you.
I've been fighting with Rex. I've been fighting with Tourette's. I've been fighting with anxiety. And I'm tired.

I stop for a moment, ready for Rhonda's voice or Glinda's to pop into my head.

Nothing. It's just me. Me and, well, God. And in that moment, in the absence of my inner chatter, in the quiet serenity of peace despite perfect circumstances, that's enough.

And so I continue.

It seems to me that I don't have to be so tired if I have a partner on my journey. I'm kind of hoping this will be You. Because . . . you know . . . You created the universe and the heavens and, from what Sam tells me, You also created me. Which means You created Rex.

And Evie.

And Nicky.

And while none of us is perfect, I'm thinking that's okay since You are.

Either You are big enough for my marriage and the Tourette's or You don't exist at all. The second option isn't really working out so well, so how about I go with the first one?

I don't know how I'm going to communicate better with Rex.

I don't know how I'm going to accept Nicky's tics.

I don't know how I'm going to raise my beautiful daughter and stop being so damn neurotic, but if I don't choose to do it your way, my life is going to continue to suck.

So, please exist. Please don't be a Santa Claus figment of my imagination. Please do something with that Holy Spirit of yours that Sam is always talking about and fill me up with your wisdom, compassion and love.

Because if you can do that, then I can love me more.

And if I can love me more, I can love Rex more.

And then he can love me more and I can feel more supported about the tics and it will all just be so goddamn wonderful.

I mean gosh darn.

Sorry.
Ugggg. I'm always apologizing.
Anyway....
Amen.
PS: Sorry to cut this short but I have to find my coupon.

***

For what it's worth, the Holy Spirit doesn't fill me with a fire so strong that I fall prostrate on the floor in the middle of Baja Fresh and start speaking in tongues. But for the first time in as long as I can remember, I feel safe. I feel protected. Call it nothing but positive thinking taking over negative emotions. I don't care. I feel grounded.

Feelings of impending doom do not hold court in the forefront of my brain. Instead, like the final scene of *A Chorus Line*, they step forward briefly, only to be kindly placed behind the true victors: joy and tranquility.

With my newly restored emotions, I sit down at the table with my children. I don't overthink what they witnessed between their father and me. In the ten minutes that ensue between the time I order food and the time it arrives, we talk about what it was – a nasty fight, nothing more.

"I'm sorry you had to see Papa and me fight so badly," I say.

"That's okay," Evie says, preoccupied with the follow-the-dots game on her placemat.

"I'm glad you think so," I say, "Because the truth is, people argue sometimes."

"Like me and Evie," Nicky adds, all the while coloring his activity placemat.

"That's right," I say. "It doesn't mean you don't love each other. It just means you have to work stuff out."

"And forgive each other," Nicky says, not looking up.

"Exactly!" I say, "Where did you come up with that?"

"From Sunday School," he smiles. "Our teacher told us that our problems are really kind of small compared to God who is so, sooooo big. And Papa isn't a Christian, so it's not really his fault that he acted so angry."

I hadn't expected such insight from a nine-year-old, but then again, in his fuchsia "Tough Guys Wear Pink" tee shirt, combined with a new head nod twitch, nothing my son ever does is status quo.

For a brief moment, instead of wishing he were like a "typical" kid, I'm overwhelmed with gratitude – for his ticking body, his ticking brain, but most of all, his ticking heart. I'm trying really hard not to cry at this point, but it's fruitless. Tears start to fall.

"Is it the onions, Mama?" Evie asks, pointing to the condiment bar ten feet from our table.

"It's not the onions," Nicky says, matter of factly. "Mama is crying tears of joy, because she feels so happy that God helps us to forgive people, huh, Mama?"

"Yes, Nicky, you are right," I manage to say. "I do forgive Papa. But what he did to us is not okay. It just isn't. You simply do not leave your family. EVER."

"I agree!" Nicky says, looking up at me with searching eyes.

"So do I," a strong voice says.

I look up to see my husband standing at the table. "Mind if I join you?"

I motion for him to sit down. "I lost my cool there. I'm sorry," he says.

"It's fine," I say, actually meaning it. "I'm glad you're back."

"Maybe you both should *gulp* … come up with a better plan … *gulp* … when you get mad at each other … *squeak squeak*," Nicky says.

I'm surprised to hear those tics again. The Intuniv had pretty much eliminated them until this moment. I feel guilt wash over me. Maybe this argument with his dad was harder on him than he was letting on.

"You okay, buddy?" I ask, attempting to mask my disappointment at the sounds.

"I'm fine," he says. "It's just my tics. They're happy to be back."

I wasn't expecting that response, but I just go with it. "Oh, are they back because you're upset over what just happened between Papa and me?"

"Not at all," he says, shrugging. "They're just happy because the drugs are no longer putting them to sleep." He grins like the cat who swallowed the canary.

"What are you talking about, buddy?" Rex asks. "I've been giving you the pills each morning."

"I know," Nicky says, now looking a bit worried. "But every morning I spit them out when you walk away. I hate those things!"

I look at Rex who just shrugs his shoulders. Before I can say anything else, Nicky continues. "The pills make me feel sad. I don't want to take them anymore."

My back goes up. "You have to," I say, setting down a boundary.

"No I don't," he says, arms crossed, setting down a boundary of his own.

Evie's sweet voice pipes in from the sidelines. Between tacos and apple sauce, she mumbles, "Nicky doesn't mind his tics, Mommy. His friends don't mind them and I don't mind them either."

"But how can that be?" I ask, dumbstruck. "I've heard kids ask you about them. Just last month at the beach someone asked you why you made those nose scrunches."

Nicky is exasperated with my slowness. "So *what!*" he balks. "I told them I have tics. It's not a big deal!"

"But doesn't that make you sad?" I ask.

"No," he says. "I'm sad that *you're* sad. But I'm okay. I really am."

I want to argue with him, but it's pointless. Something has taken over my heart. Against all my fears, logic, annoyance and insecurities over my kid's syndrome, I know deep down that if Nicky is okay with his tics, I'll have to be also. In that moment, with a million things swirling through my mind, I give the most poignant response I can think of to sum up the spiritual, mental and emotional journey that has led up to this moment.

"Okay."

And to that, Nicky responds with an equally poignant comment. "Let's eat."

And so we do.

Takeaways and Tips

- When you first start setting boundaries, be prepared to fumble.
- Letting go and letting God is not being powerless. Our vulnerability is the strongest tool we have.
- Make forgiveness your friend.
- Growth is hard work. It won't happen overnight.
- Listen to your child.
- Always eat tacos.

Chapter 20
FantasTIC

"Sorrow prepares you for joy. It violently sweeps
everything out of your house, so that new joy can find space to
enter. It shakes the yellow leaves from the bough of your heart,
so that fresh, green leaves can grow in their place. It pulls up
the rotten roots, so that new roots hidden beneath have room
to grow. Whatever sorrow shakes from your heart, far better
things will take their place."
~ Rumi

Three months later...

It's the second week of a new school year. Nicky is in
fifth grade and Evie is in fourth. As I sit here sipping my coffee
and typing this, I'm finding it hard to believe that a whole year
has passed since the initial "He has T.S." conversation with
Nicky's fourth grade teacher. Even more to the point, it's hard
to believe I survived.

Lest I come across as if I've mastered the art of Zen in
Tourette's, let me be clear that things are far from perfect. Just
yesterday my son came home to tell me that, for the first time
ever, he is being teased for some vocal ticking in class. Kids are
not as accepting as they once were of his little habits and
quirks. They are also not as nice.

The difference between this year and last, however, is
perspective. I still struggle with the ever-changing tics, but
remind myself that Nicky is joyful, witty and soulful. He's
loaded with friends, despite an increase in tics. I also know that
there's a list of things a mile long (blood tests for food allergies
. . . saliva tests for vitamin deficiency . . . traditional medicine)
that we can pursue should Nicky's view of his tics change. For

now, though, he continues to be okay with his movements and sounds, so I choose to be okay, too.

I thank God daily for my growth in this area. While I struggle with my faith daily, I know I need it. Like a muscle that must constantly be worked out lest it become flabby and weak, so goes my spiritual life. Because of it, I utilize grace, forgiveness and humor every single day.

On occasions where I fail miserably, I know I will get up sooner than before. Athletes have muscle memory. I have spiritual memory. Once hope and joy are wired into one's brain, it's simply impossible to go back to before. This means goodbye to disastrous fear. Hello, acceptance! It means fearlessly working on accepting the stuff I can't change, changing the stuff I can, and having the wisdom to know the difference.

This is not an easy task, so I take it slowly. I am kind to myself. It means setting healthy boundaries. It means not getting hung up on Rex's occasionally crankiness, but instead providing support and options for change.

In my son's case, this means encouraging him to stand in front of his class and give a presentation on Tourette's. It's unfortunate that he is getting teased for his minor noises, but it'll be more unfortunate for the kids who are informed about his disability, because if those kids choose to continue to make fun of him, they (not my boy) will play the jerk.

I don't pretend to have all the answers when it comes to being happy. I still have days when I'm so fried from Ebaying and homework and a full-time job that it's all I can do to get those kids to bed and enjoy a glass or two of merlot. (But I don't. I gave up drinking this year. That's a whole other book in itself.)

What I do know, about this God I've decided to follow, is that there is beauty and sacredness in the mystery of His ways.

Not having an answer is, indeed, an answer, and one to revere and learn from.

Along with no answers comes clarity. Tourette's has taught me that there is no such thing as perfection. There is no silver bullet. There is no final bow. It's just one continual curtain call, calling us back again and again to relive the performance. Some days the show is so amazing we get standing ovations. Other days it fails so miserably we are booed off the stage. But the main thing is that we show up and act – not as someone else –but as ourselves. As a favorite quote of mine says, "Be yourself. Everyone else is taken." From the top of my head to the tips of my toes I know my son is on this earth to make a difference as Nicky– not a shadow of someone else.

I encourage you to live fearlessly, focus on the future. I hope your own child's diagnosis — whether it be Tourette's, ADHD, Autism or any label you weren't expecting — gives you the same opportunity to accept life on life's terms. May you focus on your child's gifts, not his flaws. And may you find serenity by accepting the tics you cannot change, changing the tics you can, and having the wisdom to know the difference.

~ Andrea

ABOUT THE AUTHOR

Andrea R. Frazer is a produced television writer whose favorite characters include her two kids, husband and goofball rescue dog. When she's not thrift store shopping she's writing from her home office in Los Angeles.

48889826R00132

Made in the USA
Lexington, KY
17 January 2016